UNDER A GRAPEFRUIT SUN

Red Sox Spring Training a Quarter Century Ago

Text & Photos By
DAN VALENTI

Published by Rounder Books

ROUNDER

an imprint of:
Rounder Records Corp.
One Rounder Way
Burlington, MA 01803

ISBN: 1-57940-122-8

Valenti, Dan
Under a Grapefruit Sun: Red Sox Spring Training a Quarter Century Ago
1. Boston Red Sox (Baseball team). 2. Spring training

First Edition
2006936418
796.357
ISBN: 1-57940-122-8

All photos by Dan Valenti, unless otherwise credited. Copyright © 2007 by Dan Valenti
1959 Topps baseball card #370 printed by permission of The Topps Company Inc.

Graphic Design by Jay Walsh for www.hungryheaddesign.com
Cover Design by Ferenc Dobronyi

Also by Dan Valenti:
Red Sox: A Reckoning
From Florida to Fenway
Cities Journey
Diary of a Sportscaster*
The Impossible Dream Remembered*
Grapefruit League Road Trip*
Cactus League Road Trip
Clout!
TJ: My 26 Years in Baseball (with Tommy John)
December Sunlight
Talking on Air*

(*with Ken Coleman)

Printed in Canada

To The Divine Mercy

To Paula, my sweetness, light, and joy

To Mary V. Flynn, heart and soul of Stockbridge

To family, friends, and loved ones, past, present, and future

      And to all my mentors and teachers through the years,

living and deceased, heartfelt thanks.

Table of Contents

Greetings from

FLORIDA

Chapter I

Not "Gone Disney"

WHEN YOU STEP INSIDE a major league spring training camp, you connect with one of baseball's most essential attributes: its pace. The pace isn't slow. It's human. For when you experience a warm sun and swaying palms while the rest of the country endures the onslaught of winter, you feel exuberant and alive. You become receptive to baseball's pastoral allure. This book tries to convey a taste of that.

I took these photos while working in spring training as a freelance writer and broadcaster during the 1980s. Those years belong to another era. In 1980, baseball was closer to the late 1950s than 1980 is to today, nearer to Dwight D. Eisenhower than George W. Bush. In 1980, we wrote on typewriters not PCs, and the telegram was our version of e-mail. The eight-track, not iPods, defined hi-tech in music. It was a time when the game was beginning its transformation from a sport masquerading as a business to a business masquerading as a sport. It hadn't yet "gone Disney" but had taken baby steps in that direction.

These pictures were shot in spring training's "awkward teenage" years. Its voice was changing, and so was its

appearance. Spring camp had by then left the primitive wooden-barracks days of the baggy and wooly past but hadn't quite yet arrived in what would become today's stylized, nonstop, family-tourist-amusement juggernaut. It played out in a pimply, post-pubescent phase marked by a ravenous appetite for money and unpredictable growth spurts.

These photos, published here for the first time, depict spring training as it was and will never be again. In the 1980s, players' salaries had not exploded into the stratosphere, fans still had essentially unregulated access to the action, and the focus was on Baseball as opposed to baseball as merely another incidental form of entertainment or distraction. The game hadn't become just another way to relieve the boredom of life in an over-stimulated commodity culture. It was still an authentic, self-contained, kaleidoscopic source of wonder, in and of itself.

How it has changed. For many visitors to a spring training site today, baseball is the appetizer or after-dinner drink to a meal whose main course consists of The Extreme, Loud Amusement Park or a pampered stay at The Wickedly Expensive, Impossibly Luxurious Resort. In the early 1980s, this had not yet happened. Spring training, consequently, provided a last refuge for the hardball purist.

That's over. You won't park your car for free. You won't buy a box seat for three bucks. You won't get practically unrestricted access to players. That's why I'm delighted to share these pictures. You'll see the uniforms are cut differently, the hairstyles have changed, and the players are long gone. Each change has left a marker, though, a paint spot on the trees along the trail of memory. If we follow the markers we can come close to getting back. Through these words and pictures, I want to give you a feel for what camp was like, from the inside looking out.

Much of my work centered around the Boston Red Sox, and much has happened to the franchise since those years more than a quarter century ago, not the least of which was the long-awaited World Series championship. That 2004 title became the focusing ring that put "the big picture" of Red Sox history into proper perspective, particularly the weight of the past and the wait of 86 long years. Weight and wait. The weight was removed; the wait ended. That remarkable development, in fact, led in a roundabout way to this book.

I never believed in a Bambino's curse, but I did recognize a poorly run operation. During the Yawkey years from 1933 until John Henry and associates purchased the team in 2002, the Red Sox were run not so much as a business, not even as a hobby, but more as a vice. For too many of those years the organization resembled an old boy, whites-only, private club paneled in mildewed mahogany.

Years of being walled off from normalcy exacted a heavy toll. As a fan, even as you loved the team, you knew something wasn't quite right and it angered you. Invariably, the roster felt the effects in collateral damage that killed potential championships. Though they had dibs on both Jackie Robinson and Willie Mays, for example, the Sox refused to sign them. Wrong color. They had rights to a shortstop named Jim Fregosi, a future star with the Angels, but instead went with error-prone Don Buddin, a good ol' southern boy. Even when the Red Sox were stacked with talent (the powerhouse teams of the forties and seventies come to mind), something—an elusive, indefinable Element X—seemed to be missing.

Then the new owners came in. They ripped out the carpets, tore down the walls, and injected new life. They made Fenway Park comfortable for fans, launched what will be an eventual $100 million facelift for the beloved ball yard, and assembled a talented roster with personalities that would flourish in the pressure cooker.

As the 2004 Red Sox began their historic run through playoffs culminating in a World Series sweep of the powerhouse St. Louis Cardinals, I first got the idea of bringing the photos in this book into the light of day. The joy of finally winning a world title became the prince's kiss that aroused these pictures from suspended animation. They had been redeemed, as had everything else associated with the team's storied past.

The world championship allowed a new view of both past and future. No matter what the team had done prior to that, no matter what it would do from that point on, it would never have to look back again. The effect spilled over into the no-longer-cheap seats. Psychically, Red Sox fans would henceforth play on the house's money.

It's no accident that when Boston raised the championship banner at the home opener on April 11, 2005, the team gave the honor of pulling the rope to Johnny Pesky and Carl Yastrzemski, two guys who had endured as much as anyone. A similar impulse inspired me to bring these pictures into the sunshine.

Pesky, Doerr, DiMaggio, Williams, Jensen, Yaz, Radatz, Malzone, Monbo, Petrocelli, Scott, Evans, Rice, Fisk, Lynn, Tiant—you could go on and on. These guys had been "restored." So had every photograph in this book. The pictures can speak for themselves, though I want to provide the words that will help them do it. Think of the text as my voice-over narration as you watch the slide show.

No matter how much it changes, spring training will always be a little bit of Grandfather Baseball stepping out of the cornfield for six weeks. Enjoy these photographs in that spirit. Let us explore, then, you and I, as memory spreads itself against the Florida sky.

Chapter II

The Equipment Truck of Your Mind

BASEBALL CONNECTS WITH US because of its human dimension, limiting itself to how far a person can throw, how fast he can run, and how hard he can swing a bat. The measure fits most everybody. Athlete or no, gifted or not, chances are you've played some version of baseball.

Football doesn't allow this intimate connection, its behemoth combatants straight-jacketed in body armor. Basketball has its freakish pituitary cases rising above the rim in a way that relates not to normal human beings but to a kid pumping the controls of a mind-frying video game. Hockey delivers its icy commandos blitzing by on blades, an ice-shaved blur requiring an almost superhuman level of ability. Moreover, these three sports populate a fall-winter province.

Baseball connects in the opposite way. We relate to the game because we can play it from an early age and at almost any skill level. A three-year-old can make a decent showing in T-ball and the office worker who hasn't held a bat in 25 years can make contact in the softball game at the company clambake. There's no equivalent in the other three major sports. They remain spectacles, like gladiator fights. We witness in awe but couldn't imagine actually doing it.

On the other hand, baseball invites us in. It does so during the sweet months of spring and summer, brushing up against the most beautiful part of early fall.

As much as today's game seems bent on destroying itself, baseball still lives. The most egregious steroid scandals, the most rapacious owners, the most obscene salaries, the most obnoxious agents, the most recalcitrant union demands, the most spineless commissioners, the most self-centered superstars cannot ultimately prevent people from finding great joy in ball meeting bat.

Baseball also has the courtesy to present spring training. The other sports conduct boot camps meant to drive players to extreme physical limits. Baseball trains mainly as a show for its fans.

Does baseball exist because of winter or is it the other way around? When winter approaches the three-quarter turn, baseball opens spring training. A causes B. The emerald blades of the first crocus pierce winter's blanket, pushing up through the snow. Life comes back. Baseball returns for another year. A causes B. Hope springs eternal and spring hopes eternal. I first realized this as a lad growing up in Massachusetts, waiting for The Photograph to appear in an early February sports page. You know, The Photograph.

The Photograph was as much a sign of spring as the first robin and the lengthening days. It showed the Boston Red Sox equipment truck being loaded outside Fenway Park for the drive to spring training. The presence of this picture meant it would soon happen: the Red Sox would be playing baseball again.

I imagined the vehicle on its journey to camp. More than that, I would "make" the trip myself. At night after the covers were pulled up, I would place my alarm clock on the bed. This timepiece had a large, luminous face containing enough radium to X-ray the moon, and if you beamed it with a flashlight, it would emit an eerie, lime-green glow. I pretended it was the back lit dashboard of the Red Sox truck and that I was behind the wheel, chugging to spring training.

I drove. Little Dan Valenti, 8, Red Sox truck driver. Some kids wanted to be firemen. Some wanted to be doctors. Some yearned to be astronauts. I wanted to be one of the grunts who hauled the Sox equipment to spring training.

Once I "arrived" in camp, I assumed the persona of players. I could alternately become Frank Malzone, Tom Brewer, Gene Stephens, or anyone else I desired, and not just Red Sox players. I could be Danny O'Connell, who in an astounding coincidence had my first name. I could be Andy Pafko, whose signature was stamped in silver script in the pocket of my first baseball glove like the brand on a calf. I could even be Mickey Mantle. I loved the alliteration of his name. "Mick-ey Man-tle." How could a guy with a name like that not grow up to be a ballplayer, and how could a kid who would grow up to be a writer not love it? M-M-Mick-ey M-M-Man-tle. I savored the "m-m-m" sound, like a monk chanting "Om."

Finally, the actual van piloted by an actual driver would arrive in actual camp.

The day would boast of 72 degrees with a breeze blowing through waving palms, the sky a robin's-egg blue, and the air smelling of citrus or cactus. To a kid back home landlocked in the middle of winter this was intoxicating, the thought that while we were "up here" gritting out another cold day, baseball's "balmy balm" was happening "down there." Synchronicity, the metaphysicians call it, but I didn't need a fancy word. I was a kid. I called it fun.

Balmy balm. That's a phrase I made up, a surviving piece of Joycean childhood gibberish that attempted to describe the sunny joy of seeing ballplayers in uniforms. I liked it because of the connotations of light-headedness to the point of delirium (balmy) and the soothing relief of an ointment (balm). It also rhymed with "palm" as in trees. The Red Sox had a pitcher whose name sounded like that, Frank Baumann. In my scrapbook, I spelled his name phonetically as "balm-man."

In 1959, I was seven years old and went through two rites of passage, each occurring around the same time. The first came on May 9 when I made my First Holy Communion at Our Lady of Mt. Carmel Church. The second came when I bought my first pack of baseball cards at Palmer's Variety. I got a Frank Baumann in the first pack I ever bought in my life. Keep your tealeaves, horoscopes, hairballs, and TV psychics. From then on, the greatest omen that Boston would do well was if I got a Red Sox player in my first pack. The fresh out-of-the-pack Frank Baumann showed the lefty in a full-length pose, following through on a pitch. Surely, it meant a pennant.

Yeah, right. The '59 Sox finished four games under .500, 19 games out of first place. Welcome to the real world, kid.

But oh how I wanted to have a uniform like that. A baseball cap of blue so dark it looked black, with a floating red "B" in the center. A Communion-white uniform top with the RED on the left and the SOX on the right, crimson letters outlined in blue. Red piping adorning the neck and running down the shirtfront in parallel lines. Two red stripes lining each sleeve (no longer in the current version, unfortunately). The snowy pants with a thin red stripe down the sides leading to the best sock in baseball: a white crescent, red stirrups, then alternating white and blue stripes. Oh how I wanted a uniform like that.

The equipment van held maybe 100 such uniforms. They would be unpacked and hung in lockers. Players would arrive, put them on, take their freshly oiled gloves, slip into polished spikes, and head for the diamond leaving the first tracks in the virgin dirt, metal cleats sending divots flying back like shells ejected from a Winchester.

Photos. Lots of photos.

* A photo taken in Scottsdale, February 1961. Red Sox manager Mike Higgins shakes hands with returning slugger Jackie Jensen. The caption reads: "Welcome back, Jack." It was happening.

* A newspaper picture of Boston pitching coach Sal Maglie standing with five rookie pitchers. The pitchers, three to his left two to his right, look like extras from Zombies of the Stratosphere. In 1961, rookies acted like rookies. Their place? Keep your mouth shut and act like you've fallen off the turnip truck. The cutline reads: "HERE'S HOW—Red Sox pitching coach Sal Maglie gives a few pointers to tyros Wilbur Wood, Harold Kolstad, Robert Carlson, Don Schwall

and Darrell Massey (l to r) at Hose spring training camp in Scottsdale, Ariz. Players went through brisk drill." It was happening.

* A Bob Coyne cartoon of Jim Pagliaroni drawn for the old Record American titled "Catching on with Sox." It tells us that the "6ft3 190 pound receiver should be able to do business with that chummy l.f. wall." From the same cartoon, the team mascot says, "He could share th' series swag if our Pag hit like DaMag." It was happening.

They were there all right. The Red Sox had arrived. What was it like to walk on the field for the first time since the final out of last year's last game? I imagined it would be like the beginning of summer vacation on that last day of school, that lilting half day in June when you didn't have assignments other than clap the erasers and clean your desk. Instead of math drills and Think & Do, you attended a good-bye party, all cupcakes and Kool-Aid. You knew that at noon you'd burst through those giant double doors and not have to come back until September. You felt light enough to fly home, the entire summer still ahead.

Long before I actually made it to spring training, you see, I had visualized it in my mind—correctly as it turned out.

With certain things, one never forgets the first time: the first time you made out with a girl, the first time you tasted a toasted cheese sandwich, or the first time you walked through Ice Glen. So it is with spring training.

My first trip began on a bitter March morning in 1980 at Albany International Airport. It was a silvery, sun-splashed flight once we climbed out of the gloom, my body sustained by airline apple juice and the world's smallest bag of peanuts. About three hours later, I arrived inside the picture my mind had created long ago, in Fahrenheit-72 Land. At the

Tampa airport, I got my car and drove east. This wasn't the Red Sox equipment truck loaded with uniforms and equipment. My Alamo rental carried far more precious cargo: a long-standing desire to experience camp in person.

After a 90-minute drive past billboards for alligator farms, signs extolling the virtues of boiled peanuts, and slick ads for Disney World, I entered Winter Haven. I followed my hand-printed directions across town to Chain O'Lakes Park, winter home of the Boston Red Sox. At about 3:30 p.m., I pulled into the stadium entrance past an elderly attendant seated in a lawn chair. He looked like Gus the fireman from "Leave It to Beaver." Gus waved me in as if he knew me all my life. I followed the signs and parked behind the Sox clubhouse.

I got out of the car locked and loaded, a camera on my shoulder, a notebook in my hand. It felt good to walk around after hours in the plane and car. A dog snoozed outside the clubhouse, eyes slanted, Buddha-like. As I walked by, the eyes opened into almond slits then closed back to dreamland. If he was dreaming, so was I, but was I in his dream or was he in mine?

The air tasted like oranges.

I walked into the stadium. To my surprise, no one challenged me. No "Hey kid, where d'ya think YOU'RE going?" Expecting a challenge was a nervous reflex from my days as a lad, having been kicked out of many verboten places—in the box seats without a ticket, sneaking into the movies, crawling under a forbidden fence to retrieve a ball.

The mid-afternoon sun bathed the park in what looked like warm honey. The workouts were over. No players were to be seen. The crew raked the infield's orange-brown clay as sprinklers spit out a punctuation of water to the thirsty outfield.

I went onto the field and through a gate into the stands on the first base side, drinking in the atmosphere. I opened my notebook but wrote nothing. I left the lens cap on my camera. My behavior was counterintuitive. I had expected to begin writing furiously and to be burning up film as if I had stock in Kodak, but I didn't want to reduce the moment to words that would fall short or to a visual that left too much out. I wanted the big picture, something I couldn't squeeze in the viewfinder of a Konica SLR.

The outfield sprinklers pulsed water through hidden nozzles in bursts. "Thhht-tathhht-tathhht-ta." Da-dum five times then a pause. The sprinklers were working in iambic pentameter, the way Shakespeare did!

Beyond the right-field fence, spoiled today with development, the orange groves stretched as far as I could see. I had never seen an orange grove except in a juice commercial. Beyond the left-field wall, an orange-domed building arched in a graceful curve like a Polynesian sunset. I sat in a box seat for several minutes. Was this how the discoverer felt when he gazed at an ocean for the first time? Balboa at the Pacific? Valenti at Spring Training? Drifting came easy given the fatigue of the day.

The barking dog, though, jolted me to attention and I realized why I was there. Was the dream about to end? I walked back to the Red Sox clubhouse, opened the screen door, and went into the locker room. There I ran into my old friend, The Challenge, the loud, authoritative, "You can't go in there." Now that was more like it.

Grizzly clubhouse manager Vince Orlando, a man I recognized from Red Sox yearbook photos, lumbered over and scowled, his feet shuffling heavily across the gray, concrete floor. He was barechested, like Mussolini in the newsreels or an old wrestler, Mr. Authorized Personnel Only.

"Who are you?" he barked, his hulking presence and swarthy features looking like a spreading smudge. With a definitive "I own the place" territorial presence, he threw a pile of laundry to the floor as if to mark his turf. It's what dogs do when they lift a leg in front of a fire hydrant. A regular Welcome Wagon.

"I'm looking for Bill Crowley in PR," I said with as much self-assurance as I could muster.

"You a writer?"

"Yeah."

"Writer." He pronounced it as if he had said, "Malaria."

"Who are you with?"

"Freelance."

He huffed, clearly not impressed. He'd seen them all in his time from the biggest national outlets to the smallest rags in Palookaville. I felt like saying, "Look, laundry boy, I don't care if you've been in the Red Sox yearbook. If you don't tell me what I want, I'm going to lose my patience" followed by the Groucho Marx warning that "And I'll have you know that I once licked my weight in wild flowers." Instead I politely smiled, in no small part because he reminded me of a cross between Bruno Sammartino and Vito Corleone. Anyway, it was part of the game. There was some kind of secret rite going on with Orlando's Challenge. I never exactly caught on to what it was or learned the rules of the joust, but he was definitely testing me.

Similar occasions happened later during that first spring training visit, challenges involving a number of the team's other members of the crusty Old Guard, who for some reason seemed to take it personally that you were there, invading their sanctuary. That's how them old guys were. They enjoyed busting you to see if you'd wilt. If you were a new face, you immediately became a suspect, guilty until proven innocent. The first time press steward Tommy McCarthy saw me in the lunchroom, he rushed over ready to boot me out. I flashed him my press pass like Van Helsing surprising Dracula with a garlic clove. He read it, smiled, and said: "Ya want a sandwich?" Tommy treated me like a king after that.

"I'm looking for Bill Crowley," I repeated to Orlando. "I'm down here on assignment and I'd like to..."

"Over there," Orlando interrupted with a grunt, nodding his head to a small office across a corridor next to the screen door. Clearly, this calcified fossil didn't like new meat.

"Thanks, Vinnie."

When I called him by name, he snapped his head and looked back. I couldn't tell if I had committed a major *faux pas* or if he liked it. Didn't matter one drop to me. Orlando looked self-satisfied and dutiful. He had done his job. He had protected the tabernacle, the Red Sox *sanctum sanctorum*, from the unimaginable assaults of this, ugh, writer.

I walked to the office door. Inside the small room, an avuncular man who looked in his 60s sat behind a gunmetal desk. He smoked a pipe, the aromatic tobacco filling the tiny office with a vanilla-and-rum redolence. Long-time Sox PR chief Bill Crowley stopped his work. To my surprise and delight, he recognized my name from my first book, *Red Sox: A Reckoning*, a quirky history of the team published in 1979 and later put on the map by a reference in Dan Shaughnessy's classic *Curse of the Bambino*.

Crowley praised my book and pointed to a copy in the bookcase behind him. *Reckoning* had done its work as a calling card. Crowley reached into his desk and pulled out a blank press card. He filled in my name. The card made me good for all-access—the field, locker room, clubhouse, press box, and free eats in the mess. It was like getting the keys to the kingdom.

Crowley welcomed me, gave me that day's press notes and a media guide, and said practice would start at 10 the next morning. I wanted to pop back into the locker room and show Vince Orlando my press pass, to tell the dinosaur the meteor was about to strike, but I laughed it off. He would find out in due time.

I put my gear in the car, locked up, and walked behind the clubhouse onto a dirt access road. To my left, Lake Lulu. I had heard about Lake Lulu ever since the Sox started coming to Winter Haven in 1966. Long home runs and Lake Lulu were linked. When Tony Conigliaro would launch a moon shot or George Scott would blast a "tater," the writers and broadcasters would say the ball ended up in Lake Lulu.

I couldn't resist. I walked down to the lake through tall reeds and soggy bank, getting close to water's edge. Lake Lulu seeped through my sneakers. Well into the lake's swampy banks, the reptilian thought suddenly occurred to me. This wasn't the Berkshires. These ponds had something Pontoosuc Lake or Onota Lake didn't have. Lake Lulu had alligators.

I froze.

I stopped, looked, listened. I felt an alternate desire to high tail it out of there and to venture deeper into the marsh. It was like that moment in the horror movie when the ditzy heroine stands in front of the door—the "under no circumstances should you open that door no matter what" door. You hope she goes in. She always does.

So did I.

I took a few cautious steps almost to the waterline, walking parallel to the shore, wondering what scaly critter awaited my overtures. The lake was beautiful, small waves being driven by a mild breeze over the blue water. Water lilies with waxy blossoms bobbed on the surface better than any water show at Cypress Gardens. The plants fascinated me—vines, reeds, cattails, some kind of leafy number that looked like a cross between tobacco and skunk cabbage, a riot of wild flowers. This was the lush, tropical plant life I had seen in Tarzan movies and museum dioramas, an astounding variety of shapes, sizes, and shades.

Suddenly, as I picked my way slowly along the shore, I heard a loud rustle to my left. My heart set a record for the high jump, landing in an adrenaline lake inside my chest cavity. I was certain! It was an alligator about to lunge! I said the fastest Act of Contrition of my life and waited. Should I run or was running the thing not to do? This northern boy hadn't much experience with 'gators.

I looked hesitantly for the large reptile getting closer and closer. I watched for the angry, unhinged mouth. I listened for the ancient, prehistoric hiss. At that instant, two large white birds flapped out of their cover no more than ten feet away and flew off. My heart rang for the express elevator to my mouth. Bird words raced through my mind: flamingos, egrets, pelicans, swans, geese, Tweetie Pie, Foghorn Leghorn, Rodan. They had long, white wings, slim bodies, and yellow beaks. They rose majestically, not wanting any part of this strange creature walking the shore. I was both relieved and disappointed my encounter hadn't produced a live, honest-to-goodness alligator.

I walked from Lake Lulu feeling like Marlon Perkins and took a left onto a dirt road that began outside the parking lot behind the clubhouse. A short way down the road, past a giant anthill, I could see baseball diamonds. Of course! The minor league complex I had read about. As I got closer to the ball fields, I heard the sweet, clean sound of a ball echoing off a bat. Crack! Crack! Crack! Somebody was getting good wood.

I picked up my pace and found myself standing, set like a ruby, in the center of four diamonds. A young man stood in the batting cage from the right-hand box. He wore a generic baseball sweatshirt, uniform bottoms, sanitary hose, and running shoes. He wasn't wearing a cap. The pants gave it away. They were the Red Sox home whites. An ancient right hander with skin like parched papyrus stood about ten feet in front of the mound, throwing from the grass. A protective pitching net stood guard like a sentinel, ready to stop drives through the box.

The ancient hurler had a luminous, deep tan, like light brown shoe polish had been filtered through cheesecloth stained with iodine. He wore a full Sox uniform, though he too was without cap. He held one ball in his throwing hand, one in his left hand, and two stuffed in his back pocket. To his right, a canvas bag held a couple dozen balls. Several kids shagged in the outfield. The pitcher had a fluid motion. This old timer clearly had seen the big leagues. He was serving up meatballs, but meatballs coated with a detectable coat of major league sauce. It was great to see. A few short hours ago I stood in the freezing cold of a New York airport, yet here I was that same day watching batting practice.

Every once in a while the pitcher would say, "Nice job, Reid" or "Way to go, Reid." I had left my media guide in the car. Reid. First name, probably, although Reid was also the Lone Ranger's last name. After about ten minutes, the session ended. Reid and the pitcher walked up to the clubhouse. When I got to my car, I fished out the media guide.

NICHOLS, Thomas Reid (Reid, Nick) #51 OUTFIELDER Age 21, Turns 22 Aug. 5. Born Aug. 5, 1958, Ocala, Fla. Ht.: 5-11; Wt.: 175 pounds. Green eyes. Black hair. Bats and Throws: Right. Home: Hueytown, Ala. Signed by Scout George Digby, June 18, 1976. Length of M.L. Service-None.

1979: Earned spot on 40-man roster after a .293 season at Winston-Salem with Carolina League highs in runs (107), hits (156), total bases (227) and assists (23). Was team MVP and missed by one vote of tying for league honors. Set club stolen base (66) and run records.

The kid could hit, but 66 stolen bases? He could also fly. Oh well, the lumbering Red Sox would cure him of that. The ancient twirler turned out to be Broadway Charlie Wagner, Red Sox pitcher in the 1940s and now a minor league pitching adviser.

I got in my car and drove to the Landmark Motor Lodge to check in. After a meal at a low-rent steak house across the street ("Steak with your gristle, sir?"), I went back to my room, the orange-green-gold décor looking as if it had been shipped from the set of "The Partridge Family." I sipped an iced tea and reflected on my day. I had tested the reality against the dream and found both to be worthy. I had finally made it to spring training.

The next day I was back at Chain O' Lakes flashing my press pass like it was the Congressional Medal of Honor. This time I took out my notebook and began scribbling. And I took out my camera and began firing away. I enjoyed the sheer fun of being there. As the old Red Sox slogan used to say, "Being there is twice the fun." They were right.

Chapter III

Autumn to May

THE CALENDAR READS FEBRUARY and it looks like May. You're in Florida, a cold one frosting your hand, watching baseball. The heart sings. The refrain of an old folk song plays in your mind: "Sing, tarry all day.

Sing, autumn to May."

Autumn to May is an interesting period. Somewhere in late October, the winter wait begins. The World Series closes up its heart, baseball puts life away, and fans feel that next season their favorite team will "do it." That hope reaches its zenith in spring training. Teams get into shape, round out rosters, win a few, lose a few...and absolutely none of it matters. Hope is fed like a glutton. Your team loses? You find the silver lining. Your team wins? You use it as some kind of silly "proof" that these guys will contend.

Exhibition games serve as inkblot tests. You see what you want to see. If you squint hard enough and close one eye, you can see contention, the playoffs, a pennant, a world title. And who's to doubt it? When the last spring training game is played the stats revert back to zero. All teams are 0-0, tied for first. Your delusion will linger for a couple of months. Depending on how bad your team is, you won't come to your senses until, when, end of May? Middle of June? The All-Star break if you stretch it?

There is nothing more uncharacteristic or unrepresentative than the first two months of the baseball season. Each game is only worth 1/162nd of the campaign, and it takes an accumulation of games before the Big Picture starts to emerge. In the season's first four or five weeks, there will be a scrub infielder hitting .327 or a rag-arm pitcher who starts out 2-0 with an ERA of 2.58. Conversely, there will be superstars hitting .182 or star pitchers at 0-3, 6.21 and yet to get past the fifth inning.

Then the season gets going, game after game after game of perpetual occurrence, until finally the relentless gravitational pull of statistics takes over. The scrub is back hitting .215 and the rag-arm scrapes bottom at 2-5, 5.94. At the same time, the superstar is hitting .329 and the ace leads the league in wins and ERA. Daily the games pile up, bringing dreamers back to earth and elevating superiority to the top.

Eight teams make the playoffs. Six win division crowns. Two go to the World Series. One becomes World Champs. The rest fall short. The hopes will hibernate the following winter until that first crocus again pops through the ground.

A causes B. The fantasies begin anew. The circle remains unbroken. Until the clarity of hindsight brings the regular season into focus, until the great statistical leveling, baseball fans dream. Managers do it also, particularly in the spring.

It's March 1984, Winter Haven. The Boston Red Sox have just been hammered in a Grapefruit game. Normally after a game like this, testy manager meets truculent press. The skipper gets surly, the media turns up the heat, and the exchange becomes two-way root canal. The manager doesn't feel like talking to guys who in tomorrow's papers will be calling for his head. The press doesn't relish peeling the skipper's skin, one ribbon at a time.

It's not like that today. This is spring training. Red Sox manager Ralph Houk ambles into the pressroom, dubbed Locke-Ober South. Steward Tommy McCarthy, who looks like an extra in a Frank Capra film, brings The Iron Major his requisite can of Coke and a paper plate of Planters peanuts.

"Thanks, Tommy," Houk says. The Iron Major rolls a few nuts in his leathery hands like loaded dice. With the tilt of his head, Houk tosses a few peanuts in his mouth, lights a cigar, and lets out a chuckle in an exhale of peppery blue smoke.

"Fellas, I thought that game would never end. I was ready to play it like it was raining. I told Evans, 'Swing and miss at the first three pitches you see. I want to get out of here.'"

Houk winks at us. The Major is kidding, of course. This guy aches to win, the *marcas registradas* ® brand that marks all competitors. As I sit at Houk's table, I remind myself that this is the same Ralph Houk who has been known to peel paint off the walls when addressing smart-aleck writers. Except that Ralph is now in the mellow years with nothing to prove and confident in his abilities, a man tempered by time and also by the knowledge that he has a good ball club. He can afford to laugh at a Grapefruit stinker. Another day, another loss. Got any more peanuts, Tommy?

Houk playfully takes off his wristwatch.

"What was it Spahn said? Pitching is timing. Hitting is upsetting timing. Shit, if what we saw out there is timing, I'm throwing this away."

Another puff and exhale of smoke.

"We couldn't get the ball over the plate, we couldn't field, and we couldn't hit it. Other than that, things looked pretty good."

He laughs again and slides his watch across the table. It comes to rest next to the Coke can with a metallic clink. The Major rubs his wrist. The watchband has left a line of demarcation shades lighter than the rest of his skin. It's a relief when the manager is in a good mood after a lousy game.

"What'cha got, fellas?"

Fellas. There's something comforting and inclusive in the way Houk pronounces this word, as if by those two syllables he's admitting us into the coolest fraternity on campus. In his hushpuppy demeanor, the manager is giving cues as readily as a third-base coach flashing the steal sign. Houk is signaling us not to get our hair mussed over a meaningless loss. Keep your powder dry, fellas. The press conference ends.

To some extent, we all share the same spring fever, coaches, players, press, and fans. None of it will matter on Opening Day. This will be the year, and nowhere is that supposition more "certain" than in the spring. Pitchers can get bombed in a 14-2 game. Have another soda. Batters can slump. Bring on the Planters and light up a Macanudo. Houk is happy today.

"Sing, tarry all day.

Sing, autumn to May."

The word "spring" makes me feel fresh and alive. Back a million years ago, when cigarette companies advertised on TV, the Salem brand had a memorable spot. The ad opened with a man and a woman in a stuffy office. The young, clean-cut guy (think Pat Boone) reaches for a Salem. He puts one in his mouth and, perfect gentleman, offers one to the perky girl (think Sandra Dee). They light up. As they do, the TV screen begins to lose its mind. A transformation occurs with a special effect TV uses to indicate a dream: the screen gets wavy, like shimmering heat waves seen in the distance.

The office fades out and fading in we find Pat and Sandra in a beautiful green meadow (it's "mind's-eye green" since these are the days of glorious black and white). The blissful couple has dissolved out of purgatory and popped into paradise. They look into each other's eyes, rapturously holding their Salems, smiling their 1962 TV smiles. All is well. The stentorian announcer pipes in with a voiceover dripping with hounds-tooth:

"Take a puff [fluttering flutes] It's springtime."
Take a puff. It's springtime. That's exactly what happens to baseball fans everywhere when the calendar turns to February. Only they don't have to light up a Salem. They just have to hear two words: pitchers and catchers.

Chapter IV

Welcome to Camp Stir Crazy

BASEBALL PLAYERS DON'T TRAIN. They go to spring training. What to others is a verb to ballplayers is a destination. Put a qualifier like "spring" in front of a word like "training" and you've got the paradigm for how baseball "drills": without much of a sweat. A billion pitchers cover first a billion times and take a billion underhand tosses from a billion first basemen. Batters take endless BP. Throw in some light calisthenics that wouldn't tax a third grade gym class, get out by 1 p.m., and make your afternoon golf game. Go home to your rented mansion and do it again the next day and again the day following. A rhythm follows and reaches a hypnotic point where one workout leads to the next and every day feels the same, Yogi Berra's "déjà vu all over again." That's why players and press go stir crazy at the end of camp. They want to wake up to a different day, any day, really, but especially that most different day of all: Opening Day.

In the old days, once upon a time in a galaxy far away, when baseball players were more like you and me and less like spoiled potentates, they had to work regular jobs in the off-season to make ends meet. They got out of playing shape. Guys needed all the spring training they could get.

Open an old baseball magazine with spring training coverage and you'll see pictures of players in baggy, wooly, itchy uniforms straining, sweating, and dying to get into shape. They often wear bulky, rubberized suits under their uniforms to help them sweat more.

Think Early Wynn hanging on for one more year so he can win his 300th game. Think Enos Slaughter, 44, pictured trying to make the Yankees in 1960. Slaughter, capless and bald, looks about 100 years old. Instead of a uniform top, he wears a rubber workout jacket. He's jogging on the warning track, his face showing the strain as if his mug was a billboard for Anacin. Is that a rubber jacket he wears or a straight jacket? Is Enos bound for the 25-man roster or the rubber room? Why would a man in his right mind be doing this to himself? Four-word answer: A guy's gotta eat. Although he was a star, Slaughter probably made less in his entire career than today's 25th man makes in one season before the All Star break. The average player salary back then was $7500 year, and well more than half the major leaguers were making that amount or less.

Look closely in the backgrounds of old spring training photos. Look at the rocks on the field, the weeds in the grass, the clods of dirt in the infield. Today you couldn't get a high school team to train on fields that wretched. Some parent would file a lawsuit. Camps were Spartan. When the long day of training was done, players didn't retire to their luxury condos or rented mansions. They went back to the barracks or the team motel, no wives, kids, or girlfriends allowed thank you. Today, players rent out mansions and baseball is family friendly. Wives and girlfriends warm the bed, while kids put in as much playing time as dads.

Primitive? Listen to Hall of Famer Pie Traynor talk about training in the 1920s:

"My first spring training with the Pirates was in 1922 at Hot Springs, Ark. We stayed downtown at the Eastmont Hotel, and each day we took a trolley car to the playing field where manager George Gibson held two workouts a day from 10 a.m. to noon and again from 1:30 p.m. to 3 p.m. Between sessions, we went back to the Eastmont for lunch. There were no clubhouses, locker rooms, or shower facilities at the training site, so after practice each day we had strict orders to take a bath at the hotel in the basement. We hung our uniform near an open window in our hotel room, hoping it would dry out for the next day's practice.

"We played only 13 exhibition games, traveling by train to such cities as Shreveport, Little Rock, and Memphis-wherever a major league or minor league club might be training. When traveling, each player was given $3.75 a day for meals, we never even thought about bringing our wives or families south with us, and the silent movies were about the only break in our training routine. I guess you could say things have changed a lot."

Another photo. Boston manager Joe McCarthy, old "Marse Joe," addresses the Red Sox in the Sarasota clubhouse in spring 1948. The clubhouse looks like the barracks from the film *Stalag 17*. The planked floor is chipped, maybe rotted. The room is dingy and dark. You can practically smell the sweat, liniment, and tobacco juice. There's no air conditioning. It's blazing inside. The big wool uniforms drape over the players like a penance. To top it off, Marse Joe wears a uniform top with long sleeves. Long sleeves! Not warm enough for Joe, apparently. Reminds me of a line from Dr. Goebbels' diary to the effect that Hitler didn't like warm water. He thought it was effeminate.

The point is that once upon a time in that galaxy far away, ballplayers worked at ordinary jobs in the off-season to provide for their families. They would come to camp out of shape and would suffer through a regimen that would remind some of the Marine Corps' Parris Island, "home of the phony tough and the crazy brave."

Dale Long, first baseman with the Pirates and Cubs who once set a record for hitting home runs in eight consecutive games, would pack his duffel after the last game of the season and return to Pittsfield, Mass., where he had a factory job at General Electric's Power Transformer Division. Today, utility infielders who on their best day couldn't play catch with Dale Long make more money than the CEO of GE. They spend more on personal trainers in the off-season than Long made the entire year.

Whether you were Dale Long or a hotshot teen idol like Bo Belinsky or Tony C., you had to sweat it out in the spring. You did it in front of a sprinkling of media, a few fans (mostly cigar-chomping old men), and that's about it. Most of Florida, especially central Florida, hadn't been developed. Today's giant resorts and tourist traps were idyllic orange groves. The players trained in relative quiet on backwater landscapes. Spring training had yet to become a family destination. It was a time of greater innocence and better baseball. This hardball "ecosystem" had been in place since the earliest days of spring camp. Consequently, spring training had an allegorical status today's camps lack.

Spring training has since evolved from Valhalla to the family vacation, from an archetypal site seeped in mythos to a specific location as fast moving and transient as any produced by our hi-tech, disposable culture. Most of the pictures in this book were taken in the transition time between the one era and the other. The evaporation had begun.

In this frenetic age of 24/7 all-access sports, programming-on-demand, and the Internet, it's hard to imagine such a time. In that sense, the pictures in this book witness cultural history. They show baseball in transition from a simpler and slower era to a more complex and fast-paced age.

In the post-World War II years and into the 1970s, spring training lived primarily in black and white wire photos or in motion picture film that might pop up on TV or in a movie-house newsreel before the serial and after the cartoon. Spring training existed in a box score, in a story filed by a beat writer, in a radio report, or in the pages of *The Sporting News*, which billed itself as "The Baseball Paper of the World." To the fans watching or reading from long distance, camp existed primarily in the mind, where it was played out the cleanest and greenest.

How much spring training do players need? It's an ancient question with no ready answer. In the old days, players were there to coax rusty bodies into the readiness demanded by Opening Day. Even at that, as Stan Musial once observed, not every player needed six weeks. The Man said hitters got ready in 10 days—three to work up a set of

blisters on the hands, three to pop them, and four to build a layer of calluses.

Spring training ran six weeks not for the fans, coaches, or owners. It went that long for the pitchers, those dumb, carnivorous bipeds Ted Williams once called...well, let's stop right there. Our PC climate prohibits using The Kid's scalding epithets and a paraphrase wouldn't do them justice. Suffice it to say that you haven't "been there and done that" unless you've heard Teddy Ballgame, with all linguistic stops pulled, suggesting the many anatomical impossibilities pitchers could perform on themselves.

Ted may have been right. Maybe pitchers were "the dumbest SOBs on the face of the earth," but even the Splendid One couldn't argue with the laws of nature. Human arms weren't meant to throw baseballs. That anatomical fact has degenerated into the unquestioned assumption pitchers must be pampered.

Today, it has reached absurd proportions with the overemphasis on pitch counts, ball speed, and the grooming of pitchers for specialties such as starter, long man, situation guy, set-up, and closer. It used to be pitching. Today, it's rocket science and brain surgery. It's "quality starts" and pitchers earning a "hold" in the box score. Want to be locked up for psychiatric evaluation? Suggest the four-man rotation as a remedy to depleted bullpens or declare that starting pitchers should go the full nine.

Getting a pitcher ready for Opening Day involves time. At least that's what we're supposed to believe. A hurler is eased into throwing, first long toss, then batting practice, then an inning or two in a Grapefruit or Cactus game. First guy to go more than three innings earns headlines. First to go six and it's like man landing on the moon, which leads to an interesting aside. If pitchers need so long to get the arm built up and hitters are ready in days, why is it that when camps first open the pitchers are always ahead of the hitters? I once asked Ted Williams. Ted smiled the smile he used when he knew something and you didn't. I had walked right into it like a mouse nibbling cheese from a trap. The Splendid One said it was because hitting was a whole lot more difficult than pitching.

Any "dumb SOB" can throw a ball, Ted replied, but "try hitting a round ball with a round bat. Single most difficult thing to do in sports. There's your answer, buddy." Actually, baseball today could conduct a decent spring training in half the time, no more than three weeks, and not be the worse for it. In fact, most pitchers begin throwing weeks prior to the opening of camp. Most hitters have taken a half-season's worth of batting practice before rolling into camp.

So why isn't this done? Why wouldn't clubs train for three weeks instead of six? Today the answer is that they would lose too much dough. Running major league spring training in the 21st century is like having a license to print money. You soak the tourists for parking, tickets, concessions, souvenirs, clothing, hats, and any other money-making scheme a club can dream up. Years ago, spring training was a money-losing proposition, but the ball clubs needed the PR. What they lost in dollars they made up in propaganda.

Those Florida and Arizona datelines kept the fans' interest. Those datelines sold tickets. When you saw the words SCOTTSDALE or SARASOTA, TUCSON or FT. LAUDERDALE lead a spring baseball story, it made that gray day spitting out snow more bearable. You were coaxed into baseball.

The excitement of those datelines may be lost on fans growing up with today's 24/7 sports coverage, where there isn't an off-season anymore. Years ago, however, those datelines kept the baseball lifeline intact. You couldn't wait to read what was happening to your team down in the tropics or across in the desert. There were the prototypical stories of the "can't miss" phenom, the wily veteran trying to squeeze out one more year, the sore-armed pitcher, the manager speculating on his rotation, and so on. The headlines, wooden as they could be, provided ample kindling for an imaginative bonfire.

"Tap Sox to Run More"

"A.L. Clout Kings Spark Applause"

"Yanks' Lapses Nix Lopez Bat Skills"

"Vet Backstop Seeks Picket Post"

"Teepee Whoopin' Over Ex-Cage Ace Fischer"

"Geiger's Anemic Swatting Gives Hardy Shot in Garden"

"Chisox, Bosox Pilots' Plate Beef Triggers Rhubarb"

"Slab Staff Hikes Nat Outlook"

"Ex Dish Dud New Plate Terror"

"Cisco Kid Fills Bill on Hub Hill."

You devoured every lumbered word, knots and all.

Where is Everybody?

SOME PHOTOS STAY WITH you. A common example: the picture of the flag raising at Iwo Jima. The pictures in this book contain that possibility. A picture becomes memorable because of a Perfect Storm of factors, some contained in the picture itself and some that you bring to the viewing. For example, I vividly remember one spring training shot circa 1961. It was a black and white AP Wirephoto showing Boston infielders Don Buddin and Chuck Schilling. The picture, taken in Scottsdale, depicts Buddin and Schilling standing on either side of second base. Their hands are out-stretched, as if they were mendicants waiting for a donation.

A ball hovers in between them like a snowball out of its element. The photographer's assistant has tossed the ball there. I puzzled over this. If the ball represented a throw down to second, why would they both be straddling the bag? Isn't only one guy supposed to cover? Then it hit me. This is a put-on. This isn't game action. This is the equivalent of someone pointing a camera during a family gathering and yelling, "Say cheese."

Buddin and Schilling are saying cheese. Buddin looks the more world-weary, as well as he might. He will spend his last year in a Red Sox uniform in 1961. Shortly after, he will be out of baseball. Schilling has the enthusiastic smile of a rookie, as well as he might. He will spend 1961 setting an American League fielding record for second baseman and hit some, leading Sox fans to think they have the next Bobby Doerr. The following year, though, Schilling breaks his wrist and the Sox again resume their eternal search for the boy next Doerr, a hunt that continues to this day.

The base looks like a piece of Chiclets gum. In the background, trees ring the far perimeter. Between Schilling's legs, tiny outfielders stand in the distance. The trees make it look like these guys trained in the wilderness. Real men. Forget "Take Me Out to the Ballgame." Buddin and Schilling were singing Monty Python's "The Lumberjack Song."

My most memorable mind's-eye spring training photos also include a couple shots of Bobby Thomson, daddy of the most famous home run in baseball history. I have twice hosted radio shows with Thomson. After the second, the author of The Shot Heard 'Round the World sent me an autographed color 8x10: "To Dan—It was fun doing the show with you. Keep up the good work. With Best Wishes, Bobby Thomson." At the bottom of the photo, he wrote "Spring Training 1949 Phoenix, Arizona."

The photo hangs above my desk even as I write these words. Thomson poses in his "Lazy S" batting stance in his home whites. The uniform shows a classic 1950s cut, billowy blouse, parachute pants, socks worn right. In the background, slightly out of focus, you can see the Giants working out. A guy who looks like Monte Irvin stands at first base, back to the camera. A pitcher is frozen in the middle of a wind-up.

The remarkable thing about this picture, though, is not who's in it but who's not. The third base stands are empty. There are no fans. It seems unfathomable today, but back then, families didn't flock to spring training. They wouldn't come until the King Kong arrived at Universal Studios and the Eternal Amusement Thrill Ride lured the dilettantes with kids and caboodle in tow.

The other Thomson photo comes from the 1958-60 Red Sox scrapbook my brother and I kept as kids. Bobby, now with the Sox, is shown in Scottsdale in 1960 in a full-length shot, hands on thighs in a defensive position (he would get into 40 games with Boston in 1960, joining Rip Repulski and Gene Stephens in caddying for Ted Williams in the Splinter's final season). I couldn't take my eyes off his glove. It looked right out of the box, the orange Rawlings leather perfectly bound by light brown lacing. It had "big league" written all over it. I wanted a glove like that. Five years later I got one, a Rawlings X-PG8 Clete Boyer personal model that set me back $39.95, a fortune back then, bought with my own money, the first big buy of my life.

Again, in the background you see the grandstand. Not one soul is there. Nobody. Is this Shangri-La? The Ponderosa? The Twilight Zone? Where is everybody? That non-attendance provided more reason for media outlets to present the fans a steady fast-food diet of wire photos, stories, and spring chatter of varying artistic and literary merit. These empty calories boosted spirits and stimulated imaginations. Baseball stories ended with "notes" sections, the "Disa and Data" / "Bunts and Boots" miscellany of spring training writers would throw into a news hole to empty out the notebook.

"NOTES: Sox Mull Casale as Pinch Hitter...Manager Billy Jurges said he might consider using pitcher Jerry Casale as a pinch hitter in certain situations this year. Casale put on a show in BP. Casale looks born to hit. There's no one on the squad with more power, and that includes the earth-quaking Kid himself. One week ago today Casale hit the c.f. wall with a line drive that left a blue jet-stream. Oh, it's as far-fetched as bringing fish from Frisco but Casale, who can't get the ball over the plate, definitely can get it over the fence...catcher Ed Sadowski caught in an intrasquad game using Pete Daley's equipment. Sadowski's gear hasn't yet arrived...trainer Jack Fadden's whirlpool has been on overtime between Williams' neck, Brewer's arm, and Consolo's ankle...Jurges said lefty twirler Ted Wills might get a turn in the rotation."

That type of blather points to the nose in front of our face. It's for the fans. Such blah-blah-blahing is like burger-pit French fries: worthless in nutritional value but so delicious you can't stop eating them. Same way with the "notes." You had to read every forgettable word.

Chapter VI

The Pink of Pistol Pete

THE EARLIEST KNOWN WRITTEN reference to the game "base ball" (two words) comes in a town ordinance drafted in 1791 by the town council in Pittsfield, Mass. How much had the game taken root by then? So much baseball was being played in Park Square that the town fathers had to pass an ordinance to regulate it.

If we could take Mr. Peabody's Way Back Machine, return to Park Square in 1791, bring back those street urchins, and sit them down in Fenway Park or Yankee Stadium today, they'd understand the game being played on the field. They might die of fright seeing an electronic scoreboard or have near-fatal palpitations hearing the shattering sounds of today's PA systems (decibels on steroids), but they would recognize the basic elements of the game itself. They'd understand what was happening when a guy got a base hit to drive in a run. They'd know when to cheer and when to razz.

That's what drives us to play this game and brings us back to watch it. Baseball fans love to go back. In a world of constant and dizzying change, baseball—even today's distracted brand—provides psychic comfort, like being in a foreign country where you can't read the street signs and suddenly you see a "McDonald's" logo. It grounds you.

It's funny how one feels compelled to defend excursions into the past, as if it's a sin. The ungodly pace of the (un)civilized world worships at the altar of youth in the cathedral of Now This Moment: celebrity toxin, surface and glitz, air-headed teen divas issuing opinions on, like, you know, the war in Iraq, shallowness that doesn't have enough depth upon which to build a veneer. Time is disposable. The past is anything that happened this morning on your Blackberry. Even Pop Tart boxes have instructions for microwaving. You have to be one pretty time-stressed critter to have to nuke a Pop Tart. The past gets put down as passé.

During the 60th anniversary of the battle of Iwo Jima in 2005, a veteran of that bloody conflict was talking to a group of high school kids about his experiences in that sulfuric hell. He asked his teen audience if they knew when the battle was fought. "The seventies," one answered. "Was it in Vietnam?" asked another. The rest were equally clueless. "Don't you study about World War II in history class?"

They looked at him as if he had just said, "I have lived in this room forever" in Esperanto.

The late, great Red Sox Hall of Fame broadcaster Ned Martin fought on Iwo Jima. I had a chance in the late 1980s to talk to Ned about it. Our conversation took place in the rooftop commissary at Fenway Park, long after a game had ended. He nursed bourbon on the rocks while I sipped a beer. We got into our discussion after I mentioned my father had fought in the Battle of the Bulge in January 1945. That opened Ned up.

Ned, a literate man of great sensitivity and intelligence, talked movingly of what he had witnessed on Iwo. He then lamented how much of the past was being lost. He said memory wasn't just dredging up the past. He called it "the keeper" of the things that mean the most in our lives, both the good and bad. I was reminded of that conversation by *Boston Herald* columnist Joe Fitzgerald's great Flag Day column in 2005 about Ned and Iwo. Martin and Fitzgerald would have known only too well the old Marine's consternation before that clueless high school class.

The past is being obliterated the way the developer's chain saw laid waste to the Florida orange groves. That's why baseball may be necessary. To fathom baseball, you will have to reckon with the past, "the keeper" of what we hold meaningful.

Baseball values the past. Its statistics have the weight of biblical truths. Its old photos reveal much. You can look at them and begin to gather evidence like a forensic detective. You can use inductive reasoning to arrive at conclusions about things that might lie outside the picture. Might. That's the little word that kicks the imagination into warp drive.

As you've gathered, I often scour the backgrounds of pictures as much as appreciating the main image itself. I have two principles pertaining to photos: (1) each says something more than what appears at first glance, and (2) every photo rises above the level of its caption. A picture tells a story that spreads beyond the confines of the frame. Let me give an example from the 1959 Topps baseball card set, card #370, Pete Runnels, Boston Red Sox second baseman. It's a beautiful blend of lowbrow baseball and high commercial art (and reproduced here on page 143).

The 1959 design features a circle that frames the player's photo, suggesting halos and holiness. Maybe Topps was trying to convey a moral message, the way a prayer card of a saint would show a circle of light glowing about his head (by the way, does a nimbus keep a saint awake at night?). The player's name on 1959 Topps cards runs across the top at a slight upward angle, which I learned years later in a graphics class suggests optimism. The name is set in lower case type, "pete runnels," suggesting familiarity. Then I get it. This image is supposed to make me comfortable.

The old Red Sox logo appears in the lower left corner, a cartoon Red Sock in a batting stance from the right side. Red Sock wears a yellow headband that has a certain renegade quality (was he at Woodstock ten years after?). I love that little guy. Maybe someday he will make a comeback. Memo to the Topps' marketing people—bring this logo back; cc: to Red Sox marketing staff—acquire the rights.

Runnels' facsimile signature runs across the card. You can actually read the autograph. Guys took pride in their penmanship back then. Today autographs drip with A-list self-importance. Maybe it's an ego trip or maybe they haven't heard of the Palmer Method. "Curt Schilling" looks like the beginning of a caricature of Mr. Magoo. "Orlando Cabrera" looks like the ink lines on a Richter scale after the stylus has recorded the big one.

But notice something odd. "Pete" has signed his name "James." James as Pete? Is this like in the Bible, where Jesus changes Simon's name to Peter (Cephas), which means the rock? Is Runnels the rock upon which Mike Higgins will build his team? Not with Teddy Ballgame on the squad.

"James" Runnels. Is Pete in the throes of an identity crisis?

I thought I had stumbled onto a great secret. Was I the only kid who knew Pete's name was James? Was I obligated not to tell or obliged to yell it from the rooftops, a young Walt Whitman letting go his barbaric yawp? Was I supposed to know this Secret of the Name? If not, was my life in danger? I bet the Reds (Commies, not Cincy) would like to get hold of this information. Would I have to get rid of the evidence and eat the card? Nah. At most, I would have used a clothespin to fasten the card to the spokes of my bike, except that I never did that to Red Sox cards. Cardinal Rule: never, and I mean ever, put any Red Sox card in the spokes of your bike.

The spokes treatment made your bike sound like Brando's chopper in *The Wild One* but it sure chewed up the cards. I saved the spokes treatment for the likes of Herbie Plews, Wayne Terwilliger, Turk Lown, Herb Moford, Hank Sauer, Eli Grba, Hal Griggs, Dick Nen, Lou Klimchock, and any guy I had in triples. I was like the Red Sox in 1920. Ruthless. Harry Chiti? The spokes treatment. That'll make him talk. Harry Hanebrink? You kidding me? Clothespin him to the spokes, mister.

I loved cards that showed the player in a full-body shot. In 1959, color pictures were scarce and the baseball card was your best chance at getting a color shot of a guy on your team. I was a pasteboard purist. I didn't like the head-and-shoulder cards, and I hated cards that featured a mug shot of a hatless player. A ballplayer wearing no hat looked more like a mailman or accountant. A hatless ballplayer could have

been the guy across the street whose nearest brush with athletics was getting an annual case of athlete's foot.

Topps usually took close-ups of guys without their hats in case they got traded. That way they could still use the same picture next year without having to retake his picture again in the new uniform. Clever, but how would you like to be the poor schlep who's asked by the Topps photographer for "just one more" followed by "without the hat this time." Would that get you to thinking?

The full-body Pete (a.k.a. James) Runnels wears his visiting road grays in front of the dugout at Yankee Stadium (Topps was based in New York). Questions: why is Pistol Pete fielding ground balls in front of the dugout? Why is he fielding them with his head up? The glove is inviting with its deep, black pocket. Why is the background of the card colored pink? Were they trying to tell us something about Pete? No, that couldn't be it. Pete was a .300 hitter and later two-time batting champ. He hunted and smoked Camels.

Look carefully at the background. We can see into the dugout. There's a water fountain there. Wow! When I first saw this card I thought, "Unbelievable. A water cooler right in the dugout!" That was stuff out of *Destination: Moon*. The only water I had seen at baseball games was on the sandlot, the tepid kind with a filmy surface issued in a dented ladle from a rusty bucket toted by an uncoordinated kid you didn't trust in right field.

To the right of the George Jetson Water Fountain of the Future you can also see what looks like a vent (the bat rack?) and a protruding three-rung railing. Vents? Railings? Serious stuff that suggested engineering and blue prints, like what you'd see on an aircraft carrier or at a power plant. Engineered dugouts. This had to be the big leagues.

Standing to the right of the dugout we see another Red Sox player leaning against the railing, talking to someone. Who's the player? We don't know. We only know the player's white, and so it can't be Pumpsie Green. What do you think he's doing? Knowing Boston's reputation as a country club back then, he's probably hitting on a woman to meet him after the game in Room 207 at the Waldorf. As a kid, of course, I couldn't dream of such dalliance. For all I knew, I had sprung fully formed from the forehead of Zeus. Either that or plucked from next to the melons in the Baby Patch at A&P.

Then we see an usher. Notice the body language. Classic. He stands in a pose immediately recognizable to any kid who's ever been kicked out of the box seats. Arms folded. On guard. Eyes on the prowl for the next helpless victim who wanders too close to the railing. Ready to give the bum's rush to the most innocent, freckle-faced lad. Recognize him? Yeah, our old friend, The Challenge.

"Hey!" followed by a sharp whistle. "Let's go. NOW!" Many times have I heard such urgent notes and chiseled words only to be banished from the front row, the fall from the house by the usher. My first literary training, in fact, was in the use of the imperative mood.

"Hey kid! C'mon, get going. No hanging around here." Subject "you" understood.

For years I thought my first name was "Hey!" and felt an affinity with Willie "Say Hey" Mays.

This was the late fifties. Kids weren't prodigies or brittle as fine china. Our self-esteem didn't need artificial price supports. This was the Baby Boom. Kids were commodities, bought and sold in bulk. We weren't expected to get into Harvard by the time we were 10 or write our first symphony before getting out of middle school, wisdom many of us

same kids forgot thirty years later with our own children. In 1959, you went to a baseball game to see a baseball game. Grownups were forever reminding kids who was in charge and where you stood in the sober pecking order of adulthood's furrowed brow, which was about one step higher than an empty popcorn box. Family "discussions" ended with, "Because I said so."

Funny thing is, it worked, mostly because at heart kids crave direction and conscientious, caring parents provide it with love. Kids don't want mom and dad to be their best friends. They want them to be their parents. There's a lot to be said for that Family Values jazz.

The first big league game I saw in person was in July 1958 at Yankee Stadium, White Sox versus the Yanks, probably not long before or after the Topps photographer snapped that picture of Pete Runnels. I was six. I don't remember much except our seats were in the middle grandstand deck on the first base side between first and right, close enough to make out the ballplayers but distant enough so that the field receded into a mist of heat and humidity. It gave the tableau an otherworldly feeling, like being in a church after they anointed the altar with incense. I half expected the PA announcer to speak in Latin.

The game itself recedes in lost memory, although I can see a foul ball coming near us and ricocheting loudly off the back of a wooden seat. I remember being fascinated by Nellie Fox, and my lifelong admiration for Nellie I trace back to that day. I also remember a bunch of triples, two by White Sox center fielder Jim Landis. I can remember my father telling me how unusual it was to see one triple, let alone two, by the same guy. "You might never see that again."

Father knew best. I never did.

Chapter VII

You'll Never Lose Because of a Timex

WHY WOULD ANYONE PAY $100,000 for a Joe DiMaggio game-used uniform? Why would a baseball card go for thousands when it used to cost a penny? Nostalgia is one thing. I understand nostalgia, the bittersweet feeling that accompanies the recollection of pleasant memories. Living in the past is something else, not wistful but wasteful.

Here's the description of a 1952 Topps Mickey Mantle card from a recent auction catalog:

"The offered card has a long litany of attributes highlighted by the stunning azure blue background that seems to jump from the cardboard and hypnotize the entranced viewer! The flesh tones in the young sluggers [sic] face appear lifelike and further captivate an almost helpless observer."

Right. Whatever.

The minimum bid on the card is listed at $10,000. It probably went for five or six times that. Spending $60,000 for a baseball card. Pathetic. Loving a beat-up old baseball card because it makes you feel happy. Priceless. Here's what this "almost helpless observer" would love to do assuming I had Bill Gates' money. I'd buy that '52 Mantle for $70,000, take it out of its case, put the card in the spokes of my bike,

and run it ragged. The message would be: "You have lost your minds, people. This is a mere thing. It went for a penny. Let it go and return to your senses."

I'm opening up my photo files in this book and giving you these pictures of spring training not so you can live in the past but so you can enjoy them. These pictures aren't memorabilia but they are memorable. They are nostalgic in the best sense of the word.

"Nostalgia isn't powerful because it projects an image of a better time and place. Rather, it helps us see the people we are today and how we came to be that way," Danny Gregory writes in *Change Your Underwear Twice A Week: Lessons From The Golden Age of Classroom Filmstrips* (2004: Artisan Press). "All of those memories are the tips of the icebergs that are buried deep within us. Journeys to the past let us dive below the surface to show us more simply constructed versions of ourselves. Like archeologists scraping down through the strata of our lives, we see ourselves when our lives were full of promise, when our ideals were less tarnished, our eyes brighter and clearer."

The most resilient aspect of baseball is the nature of the game itself. It's pastoral. We know that. It sets its own pace because there's no clock. We know that too but we easily lose sight of it because of its supreme self-evidence. Football, America's true national pastime, can't make that claim. Football doubtless has other powerful attractions, especially in New England where the Patriots have won Super Bowls as if they own the patent, but football attracts differently. Football is a timed, militaristic overpowering of the senses, an assault in every sense. If football is a jet fighter, baseball is a foot-powered scooter. If football is the demolishing of a pillbox in a tank, baseball is a glide down a hill in a red wagon.

You enter a baseball stadium with the security of knowing the game won't frazzle you. It's almost beyond tinkering. The more the powers-that-be pump up the volume, the more the game rebels. Either that or at some point it won't be baseball any longer, and that day may come. A quick example is the incredibly stupid decision to start playoff and World Series games late at night. Another is the excruciatingly loud music between innings. Yet another is the growing gimmickry (the interminable All-Star Game home run derby, anyone?). There have been measures introduced to speed up the game, but baseball balks. The games keep getting longer. Yesterday's two-hour game is today's three-hour affair.

No one times a baseball game, except those wayward souls who bolt for the exits in the seventh inning to beat the post-game rush. The clock will never dictate action. In spring training, this effect is compounded since the pressure of winning hasn't been lowered yet like a boom. That will come later.

Baseball can best be understood through the grammar of pace—slow overall with five-second bursts of speed and

action scattered throughout like pepper spicing up a dish. Baseball slows us down. That's the Great Divide for baseball fans and non-baseball fans. Can you sit there for three hours without much happening? That may be the reason why baseball has generated so much first-rate literature and football hardly any. It's also why football is the quintessential televised sport and seems a lesser game in person, while baseball pretty much dies on the tube but improves in the flesh.

Lone individuals make baseball plays. You won't find swarming defenses, gang tackling, pileups in front of the net, fast breaks, or odd-man rushes. Each player on defense, the guy at bat, the pitcher, the runners on base, the coaches in the box, the on-deck guy, the umps—everyone stands alone. The only swarming defenses in baseball come from the stands, where the fans form one of the greatest mass audiences imaginable: unified, homogeneous, and susceptible, their individual identities lost to the crowd, with time to kill, asking and practically begging the performer to pull the trigger. Is that why dictators love to make speeches in sports palaces?

Baseball's equivalent of speed is urgency, for example the 3-2 pitch in the ninth inning of a one-run, late September "must" game. Unlike the gridiron (or the ice and hardwood) importance on a baseball diamond is situational and not artificially induced by chronology. Football is existential. Time ticks down, pretty much like life. Time dictates coaching decisions, what plays to run, and what defenses to call. In the end, the clock runs out. The game expires, a euphemism for "dies," forever being counted down to a fixed end of 0:00 (not content with that, hockey and basketball break the seconds into a mortality of tenths, as in 0:00.0). That is the existential dilemma, the Sophie Tucker lament baseball will never know: "so many things to do, not enough time to do 'em in."

Baseball, on the other hand, has "time" for everything no matter how long it takes. As long as you can keep an inning going, it will go. Box scores recognize this when they include the time it took to play the game. In baseball, you get as long as you need. The quickest game ever played was 51 minutes. The longest? We've yet to see it.

In 1953, the Philadelphia Phillies had a 26-year-old right hander named Paul Stuffel. Stuffel appeared into two games that year, pitched no innings, struck out no one, and walked four. He gave up a run without recording an out. Therefore his 1953 ERA is the symbol for infinity. You could look it up, as Casey Stengel used to say. Theoretically, if Phils manager Steve O'Neill had put Stuffel in a game and left him in, the game would go on forever. The clock can never run out, especially on infinity.

"Everything we feel is made of time," wrote playwright Peter Shaffer. "All the beauties of life are shaped by it." This is true up to the point where you try to capture time or bookend it with a clock. Baseball fans know this. So do football fans, in a completely contrary way.

One piece of delightful baseball shorthand is the line score, a form of notation geared toward the only bottom line that matters: who won and how. This is the line score from a game between the Red Sox and Yankees from Yankee Stadium on May 28, 2005:

	1 2 3 4 5 6 7 8 9	R	H	E
BOSTON	1 2 0 2 7 0 2 3 0	17	27	1
NY	0 0 0 0 0 0 1 0 0	1	8	0

When the Yankees came up in the bottom of the ninth trailing 17-1, they still could have won. All they needed was a 17-run rally. Don't laugh. It's been done before. Here's the line score from the June 18, 1953 game between the Washington Senators and the Red Sox at Fenway Park:

	1 2 3 4 5 6 7 8 9	R	H	E
WASH	0 0 0 2 0 1 0 0 0	3	7	4
BOSTON	0 3 0 0 0 2 17 1 X	23	27	1

The seventeen runs the Sox scored in the bottom of the seventh still stands as the all-time mark for one inning. Anything is possible.

Notice the "x" in the bottom of the ninth. When the home team leads after 8 1/2, it doesn't have to bat again. The line score indicates this with an "x." In math, "x" equals the unknown. So we will never know how many runs the home team would have scored had it been losing and come up in the bottom of the ninth. The "x" stands for eternal hope. Anything is possible.

Consider this one last line score from a game on June 18, 1961, 8 years to the date of the 17-run seventh inning game. It was also played at Fenway Park between the same two teams, the Senators and Sox. Here's the line score after 8 1/2 innings:

	1 2 3 4 5 6 7 8 9	R	H	E
WASH	0 0 0 1 4 7 0 0 0	12	13	0
BOSTON	0 0 0 2 1 2 0 0	5	8	1

In the bottom of the ninth, two of the first three Red Sox batters made outs. They had two down, a man on first, and trailed 12-5. Didn't look good, right? But by the time Russ Nixon's seeing-eye base hit eluded Nat second baseman Chuck Cottier, the eighth run of the inning had scored. The "x" turned out to equal 8. The Red Sox won 13-12. There is always a chance, however slim. Anything is possible.

Then there's the old joke of the game tied 1-1 after nine innings, where both teams scored in the first inning:

100 000 000

100 000 000

A foreigner is in the stands. He doesn't understand baseball and thinks the two teams are tied, one hundred million to one hundred million. Anything is possible.

When the Red Sox came back from the dead against the Yankees in the 2004 playoffs in back-to-back marathon, extra-inning wins at Fenway Park, no one worried about a clock. They played almost ten hours of baseball in Games Three and Four late into the cold October night. They would have played ten more if required.

That's why they probably play a lot of baseball in heaven. No darned clock up there, either. Ballplayers are limited only by their success rate. Three outs, the inning is over. String together a few hits, the inning stays alive. It's a zero-sum relationship. Your three-up, three-down is the pitcher's great inning. Your rally is their slump. The sums may always cancel out, but you will never lose because of a Timex.

This goes to the very core of spring training. Not only doesn't the clock matter; neither do outcomes. Don Zimmer used to say a good camp was playing a little over .500 ball and coming out of it injury-free. I once asked Zim for his ideal spring training record.

"One game over .500," Zim said.

"How come?"

"Because it means you've won some games but also lost enough to learn a few things about your ball club. One game over makes you a winner but you can still get the guys to listen to you when you tell them they need to work on something."

Zimmer didn't like spring training extremes. If a team racked up a spectacular spring record, there would be a "psychological letdown" when log reverted to 0-0 on Opening Day. If it lost a lot of games, it usually meant the club was a stinker. He used to say you couldn't win a pennant in spring training but you could lose one there.

Zimmer was in his last year managing the Red Sox in 1980 when I asked him that question. I loved to watch him on the field. He was a baseball lifer, a pro's pro whose heart was covered in red-stitched horsehide. These old timers have been largely pushed aside by the current fad of statistical analysis. The geeks crunching numbers on spreadsheets now rule, but I foresee a time when management respects anew things like managerial intuitions and hunches. Remember that Luke Skywalker succeeded only after he turned off his computers and followed the force.

In 1980, Zimmer struck me as bewildered and even lonely, something I attributed to the after-effects of the tumultuous 1978 season when Sox lost a big lead to the Yankees, rallied in the last two weeks to tie the Bombers, only to lose a heart-breaker in a one-game playoff. Zim would be fired after Boston's 155th game in 1980. He went about his work in the '80 camp as if he knew the end was near.

Yet he didn't complain. That's what I remember most. He took a lot of hoots from the leather lungs in the stands. In a small stadium like Chain O'Lakes, basically a lower minor league ballpark, you can hear almost every word spoken above a whisper. A few yahoos got their jollies by razzing Zim in the nastiest of ways, but he didn't react. He might put his head down for a second, and you could see him focus on a thought deep inside. A couple seconds later, he'd snap out of it. In press conferences, he patiently answered our questions as long as we wanted with that tenor voice dipped in Red Man.

Today, young fans only know Zim for his unfortunate encounter with a not-so-macho Pedro Martinez during the 2003 playoffs, and that's too bad. I liked Don Zimmer for his dignity in the face of adversity. He passed that supreme test of character: how do you handle getting thrown off the horse? Do you let it defeat you or do you dust yourself off and get back in the saddle? Zim got back up and rode another day. For that I have the highest respect. As for the mighty Pedro, he needs to pick on somebody his own size.

Great story about adversity. In Game Three of the 2004 Championship Series, the New York Yankees, already up in the series two games to none, are pummeling the Boston Red Sox at Fenway. The scoreboard shows a haunted 19-8 tally, eerily close to "1918." It's the ninth inning. The Sox are about to go down 3-0 in the series, a deficit no team has ever overcome. The crowd has thinned faster than William Shatner's hair. A man turns to the guy next to him, a total stranger.

"How come we're still here?"

"Just our nature, I guess."

It was their nature, as loyalists. They, too, had passed their test of character. Subsequent events rewarded that Bostonian obstinacy. The Red Sox came back and did what no other team had done. They forced a Game Six and then won Game Seven. By then the bandwagon had standing room only. But those two guys didn't know that in the ninth inning of the one-sided Game Three. By the rights of logic, they should have been long gone from Fenway Park that night, thoughts of baseball packed in boxes in the attic of denial until the following spring. By rights of logic, they should have been shifting their loyalties to the New England Patriots, who were in the process of winning yet another world title.

Yet those two guys stayed until the final out. They stayed when most had run away. They wanted to witness the legs of the two thieves being broken and see for themselves The Body being taken down from the cross. The Body would rise after that, but how could they have known at the time?

Faith.

Chapter VIII

Worlds Collide. Galaxies Part. The Earth Stands Still.

GRAPEFRUIT AND CACTUS LEAGUE games have the improv about them. I've seen an exhibition game arbitrarily stopped in the seventh inning because one team didn't have enough pitchers. I've also seen games extended to provide players a few more innings of work. This isn't sloppiness. This is deliberate. Baseball has had a long time to perfect the business of training, going as far back as the late 1880s, when a long-forgotten team owner had an epiphany. He decided to get the jump on the competition by practicing sooner than any other team. He accomplished that by taking his club just south enough to play a little baseball in March.

The idea caught on like Roy Campanella. Soon so many big league clubs were jumping the gun that nobody was jumping the gun. By the early 1900s, camps popped up in places like Redondo Beach, Pasadena, and Santa Monica, Calif.; New Orleans, Shreveport, and Monroe, La.; Savannah, Augusta, and Macon, Ga.; Hot Springs, Ark.; Vicksburg and Gulfport, Miss.; and Champaign, Ill. Spring training even went international, with ports of call in Havana, Cuba; Hamilton, Bermuda; and Mexico City, Mexico.

By 1929, Arizona picked up its first major league team, hosting the Detroit Tigers. Over the succeeding two decades, Arizona and Florida muscled out California, Louisiana, and the other miscellaneous sites to become baseball's exclusive training grounds. By the late 1940s, the Cactus League had taken its place alongside its older brother, Florida's Grapefruit League. Neither state has been the same since. Comparisons between Florida and Arizona were inevitable. I've talked to a lot of ballplayers about this and there's no pattern. Some like Arizona, some like Florida, and the rest don't care. Arizona enthusiasts say the drier March allows more training, and it's true. Rainouts can and often do postpone the action in Florida. Those who like Florida say the Sunshine State's humidity helps them get loose quicker. Bill Monbouquette, Red Sox ace in the early 1960s, didn't like training in Arizona because he could never work up a good sweat. The dry air would wick away the first beads. But dry heat or not, for me, the memories mattered most.

Of all my spring training moments, the one that stands out was a morning spent with Ted Williams in 1981. Williams had just arrived in the Sox' Winter Haven camp from his home in southern Florida for his duties as a minor league hitting coach. Ted loved working with the minor leaguers. They were not set in their ways like the veterans and therefore were more open to feedback. I happened upon Ted on one of the lower fields at Chain O'Lakes, the same diamond where I saw Reid Nichols hitting against Charlie Wagner on my first day ever in camp.

Ted liked hanging around down there. There weren't as many people and hardly any fans. I had wandered there one morning on a hunch, my journalist's curiosity getting the best of me. Did it ever.

DATE: March 10, 1981
PLACE: Minor League Complex, Winter Haven, Fla.

This is the day the Red Sox open the Grapefruit League schedule, traveling to Ft. Myers to play the Kansas City Royals. I have stayed behind to watch the pitchers work out under the direction of Frank Malzone. Roger LaFrancois, a reserve, is there because they need a catcher. Joe Rudi has stayed behind to work himself into shape as he recovers from a hamstring injury.

The session starts with pitcher Tom Burgmeier leading the small group in calisthenics. Some long toss follows, Dennis Eckersley pairing up with Bob Stanley, Mark Clear with Mike Torrez. Then Malzone announces the "menu"—fielding drills, batting practice, shagging, pepper, and running. It's pleasantly boring. When someone boots a grounder, the players hoot and holler ("Is that a glove or a piece of Swiss cheese?"). A dog wanders over for a siesta under a set of stands that look like they were stolen from a Little League field. After the workout is over, Clear, Rudi, and LaFrancois stay behind for extra work.

It's light and loose, but the only one who's not laughing is Rudi. Joe is pushing 34 and he's a walking question mark. The mild version of the question asks if his best days are behind him. The tough version asks if he's washed up. Most athletes dying young find themselves defeated by the odds Rudi faced during the 1981 camp, but Joe had two things going for him: his Herculean determination, and the judgment of Theodore Samuel Williams.

When I think of Rudi, an image comes to mind. I see him in Game Seven of the 1972 World Series, leaping against the left-field wall in Cincinnati to make a spectacular back-hand catch of a drive hit by Dennis Menke. The Reds' fans are stunned. He has robbed them of a victory. The next day, Rudi's catch is plastered in every newspaper in the country.

Nine years later, the famous image fades under a relentless spring sun. It's not the World Series. The nation isn't watching. This is a hard-baked minor league diamond in central Florida with a snoozing dog and half a dozen fans standing outside the fence down the first base side. All of them look like Fred Mertz.

Rudi waits until LaFrancois finishes and then steps in against Clear. He performs the ageless BP ritual, laying down two bunts, one each down the third and first base lines. They're ready to go.

"Bring it, Mark," Rudi yells out. Clear throws pitch after pitch like a human Iron Mike. The ball darts and dances, making an audible whiz as it makes its way into the plate. Crack! Liner down right-field line. Smack! A shot pulled into the left-field corner. Thwack! Single up the middle.

A ball gets away from Clear, "shooshing" over Rudi's head.

"Hey," he yells out.

"Message pitch," Malzone chirps in. Rudi looks back with a grin, the first time in the long workout that he's cracked a smile. Joe's getting into a groove. You can read his body language.

"First time I've felt good," he tells no one in particular. The dog snoozes.

Swing after swing. The sweat pours down his face in rivulets, the track of each drop a testimony to his determination to make the club as the fourth outfielder. Star slugger Jim Rice occupies Rudi's natural position, left field. Tony Perez and Carl Yastrzemski hold down Rudi's other position, first base. His only shot is to make the team as a spare part.

Will he stick? Joe's leg injury, a severely pulled muscle suffered on the third day of camp, makes the tough job tougher. I've been watching him since he got hurt. There's an inverse relationship. The more the leg bothers him, the harder he pushes. When he's not on the field, Rudi takes endless treatment from the medical staff. Red Sox manager Ralph Houk is asked about Rudi at a morning press conference.

"Well, the leg's tightened up on him, but he's working hard to get back. Man, there's no quit in that guy. Joe's in there [nods to the trainer's room] all the time."

Joe Rudi doesn't know how to quit, prompting Sox broadcaster Ned Martin to remark that if Rudi doesn't make the club, "it won't be a shame. It'll be a tragedy." Everyone's pulling for him, something that Joe knows.

"They've been great to me here—the club, the fans. I couldn't ask for more. It really gives me support not to give up."

After about 50 swings against Clear, Rudi steps out, giving way to LaFrancois. Coach Rac Slider takes the mound. LaFrancois grabs his bat and steps in from the left side. Rudi stands behind the cage, waiting for the next round.

"How's the leg, Joe?" Malzone asks.

"Still pulling but it's the best I've felt."

"Good. Take it easy. Don't push it. You feel OK? You gonna take another round?"

"Yeah."

As LaFrancois hacks away at Slider's lollipops, a seismic event occurs. Worlds collide. Galaxies part. The earth stands still.

A storybook giant emerges out of nowhere from behind the backstop taking fairy tale strides that encompass acres. He passes through a gate and loosely lopes onto the field attracted by the music of ball hitting bat. The giant surveys all he sees. Every head on the premises turns. Time stands still. The dog wakes up. Greatness arrives wearing a blue windbreaker, chinos, and saddle shoes, pretty casual for Myth.

Ted Williams, Greatest Hitter of All Time, has come to survey the scene.

The sleepy, anonymous moment transforms from ho hum to heavy, as if someone flicked a switch. Prior to Ted showing up, this has been a leisurely, Huck Finn baseball day. With Ted there, everything changes. You can feel the electricity and excitement. Even the dog gets it. He stares at Williams, tilting his head back and forth trying to understand. I get my camera ready. Ted takes his position behind the batting cage next to Rudi. LaFrancois stands in the box, looking back at Williams with wide eyes. One can only imagine what the kid is thinking. The Kid is going to watch him hit.

"Well, go ahead," Ted yells out to Slider, the giant now putting the suspended action back into play. I laugh at the sight and sound of The Splendid Splinter still barking high-decibel orders at them dumb SOB pitchers. John Wayne. The comparison has been made a million times because that's who this guy is. He is the real John Wayne. It's a cliché because it's so true.

Malzone greets Ted. Ted puts arm around Rudi.

"How ya doin', Joe?"

"Working out the kinks."

"Well, that's all right. Yes sir, give it the time it needs. You feel good up there? Swishy?" His tone is gentle, fatherly.

"Pretty good."

"OK then. We'll take a look."

Slider resumes throwing to LaFrancois. Ted's eyes focus on LaFrancois like laser beams (BOND: "Do you expect me to talk, Goldfinger?" GOLDFINGER: "No, Mr. Bond. I expect you to die"). Ted watches a few of Roger's swings without comment, but you can see him calculating the hitting geometry. Geometry? Heck, with Williams, it's way beyond that, something only he can follow. Finite absolutes? Spherical coefficients? Only Ted knows.

"Now you see what you're doing with your hands there, Rog?" Ted booms loud enough for the rest of the world to hear. "What are you doing?" The master asks a rhetorical question. How will the rookie answer?

"Dropping too much," LaFrancois says tentatively, pushing his syllables uphill and transforming the words from a declaration into a question.

"Yeah, just what we talked about the other day," Ted answers. "Here!" Ted takes a batting stance. "You want 'em [the hands] here. See? Here!" LaFrancois is aware of his mistake, and that pleases Ted.

"Good. You know what you're doing. Now get back in there." Then Ted turns to Rudi and says "Joe, I'd rather have

a guy strike out and know why than get a hit and not have a damned clue. If you get a hit but can't find the crack of your ass with both hands, it's not going to help you out in the long run." Rudi smiles. LaFrancois steps back in. You can see him making mental notes. Slider throws and the rookie turns on the pitch and lines a drive into the gap in right center.

"Keeeee-rist," Ted gleefully shouts, loud enough to bring rain or even Lazarus himself forth from the tomb. "Now will ya look at that! Look at those hands on that swing," he says to anyone within ear shot, which means half of Central Florida. "That's just what you want, Roger. Perfect. Okay, take a few more."

LaFrancois hit five more balls then he's done.

"Roger," Ted says, "C'mere." The tone is subdued, in notable contrast. It's as if Ted has thrown a verbal change up. Then I have this thought. When Ted communicates, he instinctively adjusts the form of his message to fit the situation, one of the reasons he's such a great teacher. The lesson is in full stride. I'm riffing. I'm the only outside witness as Ted Williams conducts a private hitting clinic.

LaFrancois walks behind the batting cage. Williams puts his arm around the young catcher with the bearing of a Zen master working with a novice, aware of the exact approach needed to impart wisdom. Will it be a blow from the stick or words of praise? I wonder.

"Remember before you get in the box what to do with your hands. You've got to be thinking before you step in. Them pitchers are trying to take the bread and butter away from you. You gonna let 'em? Don't help 'em out. You got a damn good swing there, Rog. You don't want to go ruining it by keeping those hands in the wrong place, right?"

Yeah," Roger answers. Williams pats him on the back.

"Now let me see."

LaFrancois takes a few cuts.

"Good. Much better." He moves Roger's hands on the bat a little and adjusts the angle of the bat on the takeaway.

"Let's see it again."

He works on LaFrancois' mechanics the way Rembrandt might apply a few corrective touches to an apprentice's canvas. Only Roger LaFrancois isn't a Rembrandt. He's strictly paint by the numbers. The thing is, it doesn't matter to Ted. He devotes as much time and attention to a scuffer as to a superstar. More, actually. It's the sick and afflicted who need the physician.

Another thing I've noticed about Ted. He loves anyone who's carrying a bat. One early morning I was standing with broadcaster Ken Coleman outside the Red Sox clubhouse. There were bats and balls lying around, and I idly picked up a bat as we made small talk. The players hadn't arrived for workouts on the chilly, misty, mid-March day.

Ted arrives. He walks up to Ken and they begin talking. Ken introduces me to Ted, the first time we were formally given the honors. Ted sees my bat.

"Let me see your swing."

Now I know how a maple tree feels when it's zapped by a lightning bolt.

"Really?" I ask, not believing this.

"Yeah. Let me see your swing." Ted Williams is nothing else but literal when he's talking about hitting. If he asks to see your swing, he honestly wants to see it. I assume my stance in a phantom batter's box. The imaginary pitcher comes in and I take a cut.

"You got a nice little swing there." That's Ted's stock response to every swing he sees owing to his cardinal rule:

never change a guy's swing. "Yes sir, I like it."

Is he humoring me? If so, I'm eating it up. Then he has me swing again. No. He's not humoring me. He's studying me.

"Who'dja like as a ballplayer?"

"You."

"Aw, shit," Ted replies in a half laugh, half needle.

"No, I mean it. I liked you."

"You're not old enough to have seen me play," he challenges.

"Oh yes I did," I shoot back. Ted smiles.

I then tell him the story of how I was in the box seats right behind the Red Sox dugout with my father and brothers on Sept. 27, 1960, the penultimate game in The Kid's career. Everybody remembers his last game the next day and Ted's legendary home run off Jack Fisher in his final career at-bat. Nobody remembers the day before, with just cause. The Orioles pummeled the Sox 17-3, though Don Gile hit a home run over everything in left for the Sox (you take solace where you can find it).

After each half inning, when Ted ran to the dugout from left field (incidentally touching the first base bag each time), I would lean on the dugout, waving and yelling, trying to get his attention. Why? I wanted him to look at me. I figured that seeing me would be acknowledging me. What the acknowledgment would mean I hadn't a clue, but driven by a subconscious impulse I felt compelled to try to flag down the Thumper's attention.

Actually it was hard to say anything because that same morning, on the last tollbooth on the Mass Turnpike before coming into Boston, my dad's 1958 Ford Fairlane was rear-ended. My head slammed into the back of the front passenger seat, splitting my right upper lip wide open. I ended up at Massachusetts General Hospital, where a green-gowned doctor stitched my lip. It was a lot to go through, especially for my father, but we finished at the hospital in time to get to Fenway Park in the second inning. It's one of the greatest memories of my dad, that he took us to the game despite the accident and all he had on his mind. He did it because he knew how much it meant to his kids. Such an action is worth a million "I love yous."

Ted likes the story.

"Your dad took you to the park after that? Well, you got one helluva good father there. And you were down there [behind of the dugout]?"

"Yep. I just wanted to see you and have you look at me."

"Well, I'm looking at you now. How d'ya like it?"

"I like it just fine."

He laughs, and then has me swing again. He sees something.

"Here."

Ted gets behind me, puts his arms around both my hips, and tells me to take another cut. I do, but the vice-like grip from Ted's big, powerful hands keeps my hips from rotating.

"See that? You can't generate anything without your hips. Try it again. See? That's what I mean when I tell these guys, 'hips before hands.' You need to open up your hips before your hands come around. You're not opening up. Try it now but get your hips out front."

I swing again, trying to get my hips to fly open.

"That's better. Hips before hands. Yeah, that's a lot better. Don't you think, Kenny?"

Coleman agrees, saying that if I keep it up, the Sox might want to sign me.

"Yeah," I say, playing along. "I'd be a table-setter. Nellie Fox type."

"Fox. Helluva ballplayer. Could beat you in a lot of ways. Smart. Knew infield play. Knew how to get on base. That's why I took him with me to the Senators," Ted says, referring to his decision to add Fox to the coaching staff when Ted managed in Washington. "Look, you don't have to be big to play ball. Little guy like you, if he can learn to get on base and play the field, you got a place in this game."

"Like Dommie and Johnny," Coleman adds.

"That's exactly right." Ted adds that a lot of "big guys" might have inherent strength and power, but too many "didn't learn discipline at the plate. Then you got a guy like Fox. Knows the strike zone. Makes the pitcher work. Works a walk, slaps a ball the other way, lays down a bunt, goes up the middle a lot. He's gonna beat you. Don't need size. No sir."

I probably had a couple dozen encounters with Williams during my years at spring training. Having a bat in my hand the day Ken Coleman introduced me to Ted put me on to my "secret weapon." Even though Ted had mellowed by that time, what Winston Churchill called "the black dog" could still bite him. Being a writer also didn't improve my odds. I had heard about Ted's legendary dark moods that could come on in a foul flash, and I didn't want first-hand experience. So I had a trick. I'd find a bat lying around and would approach Ted, holding the stick in my hand. Ted caught on, though, and took delight in ragging me about how a young guy needed a "walking stick." Nonetheless, it became a running joke and my little "in." He started calling me "the old man," never missing a chance to get out the needle. One time, he saw me without a bat in my hand.

"Hey old man," Ted boomed. "Where's your cane?"

I replied, "If I'm old, that makes you Methuselah." Ted roared and came back, firing.

"Yeah, and I've got as many damn aches and pains, but I sure as hell could out-hit him." Nobody got the last word on Ted Williams. And so it became: I was the "old man" and he was "Methuselah." If Ted liked you, he needled, not hesitant about pouring it on, and he absolutely loved guys who could give it back. I never had a sour encounter in all my time with The Kid nor did I see a trace, thankfully, of the dreaded "black dog."

Back at the batting cage at the minor league complex in Winter Haven, Joe Rudi steps in the box, cracking lines drives.

"That's it, Joe. Up the middle. Attack it up the middle," Ted yells. More balls are sent to their appointed rounds in the outfield and over the fence. Then Rudi swings and misses. Then he fouls off the next pitch. As he follows through, he grimaces and shakes his head. Williams picks up on it instantly. He has seen something. I wonder how he's going to approach the veteran. It's one thing with LaFrancois, a rookie, but how will Ted handle the former All Star?

"Joe, let me ask you a question. Why are you dropping your head back at the end of your swing? You did it on those last two swings."

Rudi says he didn't realize the movement. No one else saw it either, but Ted did, and if Ted sees something that 99,999 people miss, it means it's there and the rest of us are blind.

"Take a swing, Joe." Rudi takes a cut. "Did you feel it?"

"Yes," Rudi answers.

"Take another swing. Watch the head this time."

Rudi cuts.

"Better?" Ted asks.

"Lots."

"Okay, get back in there. C'mon, Rac, we ain't got all day."

Slider delivers and Rudi sends the next pitch out of the park.

"See that?" Ted excitedly asks the world. He's like a little kid in his enthusiasm. Rudi nails a couple more balls. "Ya see the way he's driving that ball? Whoa, baby! Ha, ha!" Ted's getting a kick out of this. When Rudi steps out of the cage again, he talks with Williams.

"Nice job, Joe," Malzone says.

"Thanks, but it still feels a little slow," Rudi answers.

"That's OK," Ted says. "Yes bat speed is important, but that will come. Just be quick. Be quick! Be quick with the hands. Bat speed will come. Quick first then speed." Ted then delivers a post-graduate lecture on the difference between bat speed and hand quickness (the latter is the more important and determines the first). The linguist in me stands in rapt attention at this fine job of parsing. The hitter in Rudi looks on in awe.

"Joe, you've got a damn good swing. You don't ever have to worry about that. But Jesus, don't give them pitchers any more advantage than they already have. Pitchers will scratch their ass and pick their nose but most of them won't know how they got you out. The truth is, they get batters out because hitters help them too much. That's why when you start moving your head or holding your hands in the wrong place, you're taking money out of your own wallet. Here."

Ted takes an imaginary bat in his hands and swings viciously—but with total purpose and economy of movement—at an imaginary pitch. He stops his swing at various points, annotating with commentary. At this moment, I feel chosen. Ted Williams is breaking down his own swing for Joe Rudi and me.

By this time, the rest of the workout is long past over. Everyone else has headed up to the clubhouse except Rudi, Malzone, Williams, and me. Ted continues to demonstrate his classic swing, offering verbal notes on hand position, balance, stride, and hip action. He infects us with three topics: hitting, hitting, and more hitting.

"I can tell you this, Joe. Don't let them change your swing. In all the years I've been talking hitting to players, I've never messed with a guy's swing. Is that right, Malz?"

Malzone nods in agreement then wags a line that brings out a huge horselaugh from Williams. "Except Bobby."

Frank means Bobby Doerr, the great Red Sox Hall of Fame second baseman. For decades, Ted and Bobby have had a running feud on hitting theory, all in good-natured, needling fun.

"Well, okay, if ya want to get technical on me," Ted says after his belly laugh dies down. "Except for Bobby. I'll grant you that. But you gotta give me this. He sure as hell needed it. You gotta give that to me." Vintage Ted, the consummate polemicist, getting in the last zinger. "I can honestly say this. All the players who I instructed and talked to during my career playing and managing have all become better hitters. Now some people will start saying 'There goes Williams again, shooting off his mouth,' but the record will bear that out. Just look at what happened when I managed in Washington, how them averages went up. Jeeezuz, Joe, you've got the best swing in camp. I can't buy them wanting to mess with it."

Williams' last remark refers to advice Rudi's been given by Sox hitting coach Walt Hriniak. Ted hated the Charley Lau-Hriniak theory of hitting. There was nothing on earth as inelegant as the Lau-Hriniak swing, the batter standing on the wrong foot, swinging down on the ball, and letting go of the bat on the follow through. I used to call it "the helicopter chop." That butt-ugly swing helped some players (Dwight Evans) and hurt others (Rich Gedman). It clearly wasn't doing wonders and spitting cucumbers for Joe Rudi. With Williams' blessings and to Hriniak's consternation, Rudi went back to his natural swing and started tagging the ball.

"Well, I tried it [Hriniak's way] but it didn't work. I'm back to what got me here and it's the first time I've hit the ball well."

"There you go," Ted answers, delighted. "Joe, it's not the swing. The single most important aspect in all of hitting is getting a good pitch to hit. Up until two strikes, you can afford to be selective. You make that dumb bastard work to get you out. You hit your pitch. Now let me ask you this, Joe. What pitch gives you the most trouble? Show me."

Rudi takes his stance and indicates with his right hand an area high and inside.

"Okay, then. Up until two strikes. Lay off it. You get selective up there, Joe, and you'll be looking at more 2-0, 3-1 pitches than you ever have before. Okay, now let me ask you. What pitchers give you the most trouble?"

"A lot," Rudi laughs.

"Name one."

"[Jim] Palmer."

"When he first starts you off, are you looking for a slider or a fastball?" Ted asks.

"It depends."

You can tell by Ted's face that he's not satisfied with the answer but he doesn't say so. Instead, he takes the indirect approach. He illustrates it with a story.

"Let me tell you something. The day of the Red Sox-Yankee playoff in '78, Yaz came to me and said he'd be looking for sliders from Guidry all day. I said 'Damn it, Yaz. He's not going to throw you sliders right off. He'll go with his fastball. If it gets late in the game or if he gets in trouble, he'll use the slider. But the first time up, you've got to look for a fastball!' Well, Yaz comes up for the first time. Sure enough. Guidry threw a fastball and damned if Yaz didn't put it out. Joe, this is hitting, from here [touches his neck] to here [taps his forehead]."

Ted Williams, living monument, is once again proven correct. The Hriniak "copter chop" swing was earning Rudi a one-way ticket to an outright release. Rudi would have "coptered" his way off the ball club. Once he listened to his own instincts and found a papal blessing from the Splendid Splinter, Rudi began hitting. He made the team and stuck all year.

The Kid pontificating on hitting. Is that a moment or what? It was without question the most satisfying aspect of my jaunts to spring training—getting to meet and have a bit of a relationship with Ted Williams.

Chapter IX

So Much Depends Upon

ON THE DAY AFTER Ted's hitting lesson with Joe Rudi, the Red Sox play the home opener against the Tigers. The players take the field shortly after 10 a.m. for batting practice and running. At about 11 a.m., a bunch of players not in the starting lineup head to the minor league complex with coaches Johnny Pesky and Rac Slider for hitting.

Pesky divides the eight hitters into two teams of four apiece. Reid Nichols, Chico Walker, Julio Valdez, and Roger LaFrancois make up the Red Team. They will be facing the Blue Team consisting of Garry Hancock, Tom Poquette, Rich Gedman, and Dave Schmidt. They play a game that reminds me of the informal pick-up games we used to play on the sandlots except that these guys are big leaguers, an irony that delights me.

The "game" goes nine innings, with five outs per half inning. Slider pitches and Pesky umpires. Pesky keeps score and "announces" the game. The players' competitive juices take over.

"Blue Team is ahead, 4 to 3," Pesky reports. "One out, Red Team. You've got a chance to tie the game. Let's see what Pork Chop can do here." Pork Chop is Chico Walker.

"All right, Tom. Men on second and third."

They are the same imaginary men we used as kids.

"Get them runs in."

The innings fly by. After it's over (Blue Team wins 11-10) the players thank Johnny, who has had the most fun of anybody.

"Aw, what are you guys talking about? I didn't do anything," Pesky says. Johnny's such a great guy he can't even fake a convincing grumble. Later that day, the Tigers soundly beat the Red Sox in the Grapefruit League home opener. Houk's press conference after the game is upbeat and loose. Cuisine is Coke and Planters.

WRITER: What about Remy and Stapleton, Ralph? Do you know who will be starting at second?

HOUK: Let's put it this way. They'll both play a lot.

WRITER: What about Dorsey?

HOUK: He looked good for his first time out. I thought his curve ball was better than expected.

WRITER: What are your plans for Miller?

HOUK: Well, Miller's our center fielder. The main thing I'm looking for in center is defense. I don't think we'll lose anything at all with Miller out there. He can go get 'em.

WRITER: How many outfielders will you take north?

HOUK: More than likely we'll take five. But as I've said all along, I don't make these decisions. The players make the decisions for me.

WRITER: Do you think Valdez will back up Hoffman?

HOUK: I've only seen Julio play five innings, but I've heard some very good things about him. He can make the great plays at short, he's a switch hitter, and he has good speed. That's a pretty good combination there.

WRITER: How about Evans? Do you think you'll be using him a lot at lead off?

HOUK: I think so. He's a good leadoff man. Look at his on-base percentage. Last year it was one of the best in the league. Speed isn't the only thing you look for in a leadoff hitter. You need someone who knows how to get on base. That's what Dwight does. He makes pitchers pitch.

Houk's casual manner seems perfectly reflected in the words "spring training," a delightful adjective modifying a rigorous noun. The noun is regimental, like a close-order drill. The adjective is pastoral, like a picnic with your girl. Put the words together and you've got chemistry. The interaction produces a unique effect, opposites attracting to such a degree that they cease to be opposites. The words aren't seen anymore as two different parts of speech but as a phrase, an interconnected grammatical unit.

"Spring" is Athens. "Training" is Sparta.

"Spring" is Palm Springs. "Training" is Death Valley.

"Spring" is mom waiting for you with cookies and milk. "Training" is a drill instructor tossing you a cold MRE.

"Spring" is June Cleaver. "Training" is Joan Crawford.

Combine them and something wonderful happens. Spring Training.

On and on it goes. Managers "feeling good" about the way the team looks. Players believing they're ready to "kill it," meaning to seize the moment by having a huge year. Fans lost in the dream of it all.

A truism about baseball fans. Their patience has a long radioactive half-life. They are impatient with the pitch but long suffering for the at-bat, critical during the inning but understanding over the game, doubtful for the game but sympathetic for the season, cynics for the season but loyal for a lifetime.

I'm glad you had the chance from these pictures and words to get a taste of what it was like. I went to spring training for 10 years. All the duties and deadlines in the world, all the temporary setbacks and obstacles, were never able to pull ahead of the fun. The responsibilities never caught up to the reverie. These photos prove that. How could it be otherwise? There stood I, that baseball-crazy boy grown up to be an adult, getting paid to hang around big league camps.

Every day I spent in spring training, I felt like that little kid in bed "driving" the Red Sox equipment truck and eventually arriving under a grapefruit sun.

With apologies to William Carlos Williams:

> *so much depends upon*
> *a red sox player*
> *glistening with spring sweat*
> *standing beside the white-chalked batter's box.*

So much depends upon spring training.

Chapter X

Appendices (Spring training interviews with Boggs and Clemens)

Wade Boggs (spring 1982)

"Man, I just love to hit. That's the simplest way to explain it."

I conducted this interview with Wade Boggs in spring training 1982. Who was Wade Boggs back then? Nobody, that's who, a complete unknown laboring in obscurity, just another rookie trying to make the club. At the time of our interview, Boggs had never set foot in Fenway Park. He had been stuck in the Boston farm system for the previous five years. He hit well everywhere he played but that spring was listed as a long shot to make the team. We chatted in early March, long before the mainstream media gave two seconds to Wade Boggs.

Boggs was signed as a seventh round pick in the 1976 draft after an All-State and All-American career at H.B. Plant High School in Tampa, Fla. In 1981, he won the International League batting championship. This led to a promotion to the 40-man roster and an invitation to the Boston spring training camp in 1982. He made the 25-man roster when the team broke camp and hit .349 in 1982, setting the all-time rookie batting mark. He went on to become one of the game's best hitters. Boggs was elected to the Hall of Fame in 2005. That was all ahead of him when we talked in camp. This interview is likely the first Boggs ever gave wearing a major league uniform.

DAN VALENTI: What are your chances of making the ball club?

BOGGS: I think they're fairly good, whether or not it's backing up Carney [Lansford] or Stape [first baseman Dave Stapleton] or DH-ing a little bit or pinch hitting. Of course, you never know about stuff like this. They may want [to keep] me or they may want to send me down. And to be honest, I'm not really sure what I would want to do: play every day at Pawtucket [the Sox Triple A farm team] or stay up with the big club and ride the bench. I honestly don't know. I've tossed and turned that one in my mind just about every night, when I'm lying in bed trying to get to sleep.

VALENTI: But if it came down to a choice—one or the other—what would you prefer at this point in your career?

BOGGS: I guess I'd rather play every day at Pawtucket. A lot of guys say it's best to be up here getting the exposure, because being in the big leagues is where it's at. But I don't think I'm the kind of ballplayer who can just sit around. I've gotta be working. I have to be out there on the field contributing. I love the game so much. I have to be involved in it. I think playing every day will keep me sharp so that when the time comes for me to make my mark on the Boston Red Sox, I'll be ready.

VALENTI: Your track record has been one of consistent .300-plus seasons in the minors. Do you think there will be much of an adjustment hitting major league pitching?

BOGGS: No not at all. In fact, I think it will probably be better to hit up here, much easier, because of the better lighting, the better parks, and the hitting backgrounds. Also the infields are manicured a lot more professionally than they are in the minors and balls go through the infield faster. For a line-drive hitter like me, that will produce additional base hits. Of course, they also make better defensive plays up in the big leagues. But overall I think it will be easier for me to hit. Another important thing is that the pitchers in the majors are always around the plate. For my style of hitting, this is a definite advantage.

VALENTI: I'm sure you've heard a lot about Fenway Park, but have you ever actually been there and hit there?

BOGGS: No. I've never set foot in Fenway Park, but I've seen it on TV and I'm familiar with how the park is built. Plus I've talked to guys who know the park well, guys like Ted Williams, and I'd say Fenway is well suited to my style of hitting because I inside-out the ball a lot and go the opposite way. I hit the long fly balls to left center, and I can also pull the ball. So if the pitch is away, I can hit it off the Green Monster in left. If the pitch is inside, I can pull it down the line or shoot the gap. Because the park is asymmetrical, I think it will help a hitter like me who can use the whole field. Fenway has short lines, 380 in the gaps, 420 to center. There are also a lot of ins and outs, the nooks and crannies you hear about like the triangle in center, the deep part in right, the wall in left. It's just to your benefit if you can use the entire ballpark. The other thing that encourages me is that Boston has had a history of successful left-handed hitters.

VALENTI: Yes. If you look back, you'll see batters such as Ted Williams, Billy Goodman, Pete Runnels, Yaz, and Fred Lynn. All were batting champions. Even Bernie Carbo had great success in Fenway because of that inside-out swing that you just described.

BOGGS: Those were some great hitters that you just mentioned, but I would categorize myself more as a George Brett-style of hitter. For example, if the pitch is away, I can go out and get it and go that way. If they break off a slider down and in or a fastball up and in, I can turn on it. This is hitting Brett-style. I think all the hitters you mentioned could do that. Even Ted. People say he didn't hit to left field enough, but he did, especially late in his career. That style of hitting is tough to defend against. Next thing you know, the defense is trying to stack up in certain ways, like the [Boudreau] shift they had for Ted. That just opens up other things for you as a hitter.

VALENTI: How would you defend Wade Boggs in the field?

BOGGS: That's a great question, and the honest answer is I wouldn't know. If you play me to pull, I'll go away. If you play me the other way, I'll pull. If you play me straight away, I'll work the gaps. One thing I work very hard on in batting practice is those kinds of situations and ball placement. I'll try to put the ball in play to certain spots, depending on the defense and the pitch. That's why every at-bat is different, the way Ted said in his book [*The Science of Hitting*]. Each at bat is an opportunity to learn something. The good hitters take all they learn from every at bat and apply it to the next one. That's what I try to do.

VALENTI: One of the hitting exercises I've noticed you do is to get in the batting cage and have someone toss you the ball underhanded to hit. Seems like anyone could hit an underhand toss. Why does a professional hitter do that?

BOGGS: It's done mainly to teach you how to stay on the ball, all the way from delivery, to contact, and into the follow-through. This exercise also teaches you bat control. It's an excellent way to practice driving the ball the other way or pulling the ball. I know it seems like that couldn't be with the pitch coming in so soft, but it doesn't matter how the ball gets there. All that matters is that it's there. That's what people may not understand if they see that type of drill. The big thing in a swing is the point of contact and what you do with it in terms of bat meeting ball. If you can control where your bat sends a ball in that exercise, you can do it against live big league pitching. The other thing that exercise does is help establish my hitting rhythm. You can get your timing down a lot better with the underhand toss than you can by taking batting practice. I think more guys ought to do this exercise. Many do, but not enough of it. I guess it's not macho enough [LAUGHS].

VALENTI: Yeah, we hit underhand pitches when we were in grammar school. I probably led the third grade in batting.

BOGGS: Right. It doesn't look like a big league hitter would get anything out of it, but I sure do.

VALENTI: Is this your first spring training with the parent club?

BOGGS: Yes it is.

VALENTI: What's it like coming here for the first time?

BOGGS: It's awesome! You just can't say enough about it. I spent my last five spring camps with the minor league clubs, training down on the little fields [the minor league complex]. Now I find myself at last up here, playing with my idols. Like yesterday, I got to see George Brett hit in an exhibition game. It's just phenomenal to watch him hit like that, not as a fan but as a colleague more or less. Now I find myself around these guys every day, guys like Rice and Yastrzemski, for example. You train with them. Have lunch with them. Talk to them. It's the only place to be.

VALENTI: Do they accept you? Guys like Johnny Pesky and Frank Malzone say that when they were coming up years ago, it was a lot different for rookies. They came in, kept their mouths shut, and did what they were told. Malzone says that in his rookie camp in the mid-1950s, he got a grand total of one at-bat all spring and that it was hard to even find time for batting practice. How do you find it now?

BOGGS: It's totally different. They've made me feel at home. I go into the clubhouse and I walk by Eck [Dennis Eckersley] and say "Hi" and he says "Hi" right back. And there's usually kidding, razzing, that sort of clubhouse stuff that lets you know you're accepted as one of the guys. And that's what it's all about. We've got a great bunch of guys on this club, and there are no snobs—you know, the kind of guys who slough you off if you say hello to them. I'm with a terrific bunch of guys.

VALENTI: Wade, you're part of baseball history. Last year [1981] you played in the longest game of all time, the

33-inning game at Pawtucket that began on Easter Sunday and concluded June 23 after eight hours and 25 minutes of baseball. Go back to that game and give me your thoughts on making baseball history.

BOGGS: It was incredible. We were into the 11th inning and Rochester had a man on second. I made a diving play in the hole at third and threw the guy out, saving a run. At that point, it was about 31 degrees. It was windy and freezing. That game just kept progressing, and Sammy Bowen hit one for us that under normal conditions would have been way over the light tower for a home run. That was in the 19th inning. We all thought it was gone and we ran out on the field to congratulate him, but the wind got the ball and blew it back and the left fielder caught it.

VALENTI: Okay, that was the 19th, and Rochester scored not long after that.

BOGGS: Yes. In the top of the 21st inning, Rochester scored a run. We thought the game was over, but we came up in the bottom of the inning, and Dave Koza led off and popped one up to center. Then the wind caught it and kept blowing the ball in and to the right and the ball fell behind the first baseman. The wind was blowing at about 25 mph, swirling all around, and the chill factor was something like five degrees. Well, I came up and hit a fly ball also to center, and it blew over to the left field line and fell in for a double. That drove in Koza. A couple of wind-blown balls that should have gone for outs. At that point, we were saying, "Gosh, this can't go on. Somebody's got to score and win it." It got to the 25th inning, and I made another diving stop with a guy on second and saved the game again. At that point, I said to myself that this game will never get over. At that point, it was after three in the morning. There was a 12:50

a.m. curfew, but the umpire ignored it. They had to call the league president. Meanwhile, the game continued until it was suspended at 4:07 a.m. It was just incredible.

VALENTI: So the game goes to the 32nd inning, then it's suspended and continued on June 23rd, right in the middle of major league baseball's players' strike. This meant that media from all over the world showed up at McCoy Stadium for the resumption of play.

BOGGS: It was a circus. That's the perfect word for it. I've never seen so many sportswriters and media people congregated in one area in my entire life. They were there from all over the United States, from Hong Kong, from China, from England, from everywhere. And everybody wanted to ask you questions. It was unreal, Twilight Zone stuff.

VALENTI: When the game ended in the 33rd with Marty Barrett scoring the winning run, was there a sense of relief that the resumption had only lasted one inning or did you guys want to see it go on?

BOGGS: Well, the fans wanted to see it go another eight or nine innings and I think the press wanted it to go on some more. They thought, well, geez, you've gone this far. Let's see how many more innings you can tack onto it. The game had taken on a life of its own. It was almost as if it was alive, like on one of them old monster movies. They wanted to see it grow and keep getting bigger. But I didn't really care. Just winning the longest game in baseball history was a thrill because that game will always be remembered.

VALENTI: Getting back to your position with the Red Sox, do you have any goals for yourself going into the 1982 season?

BOGGS: Just one, and that's to better myself over the course of the year. If I have to go back to Pawtucket, I'd like to shoot for a .400 season because I've had so many .300 years in a row. If I stay up here, I want to hit .300.

VALENTI: Do you think you could hit .400?

BOGGS: Well, shooting for .400 would be more of a challenge. To hit .400—in the big leagues, in the minors, in high school, anywhere—you'll need a lot of luck. And when you get up 500 to 600 times, you're talking around 240 hits. That's difficult. You'll also need to stay completely healthy and have a hitting style that hits to all fields with occasional power to keep the defenses honest.

VALENTI: Sounds like you just described Wade Boggs.

BOGGS: Actually, I was describing George Brett, but I don't mind the comparison.

VALENTI: Has hitting always come natural to you or is it something you had to work at?

BOGGS: I guess I'm a natural hitter, if there is such a thing. But I have to explain that. I say "natural" to mean that when I was a young boy, I found I could handle a bat. It came easy to me. A bat felt comfortable in my hands, from the first time I ever picked one up. My father was very instrumental in recognizing this, and he worked with me a lot. My dad idolized Ted Williams, and I'm sure he used some of Ted's ideas on hitting with me. But to say I was a natural doesn't mean that I didn't work every day on my hitting. I did back then and I do it today. When we are at home during the course of the season, I'll take 45 minutes of extra batting practice. A lot of guys frown on this and say it's going to wear me out come August, but it doesn't. It really makes me a stronger hitter. And it doesn't hurt that I love to hit. Man, I just love to hit. That's the simplest way I can explain it.

Roger Clemens (spring 1984)

"I'm not David Clyde. He wasn't Roger Clemens."

One of the regularly appearing characters of spring training is "The Phenom." The label refers to a hotshot kid who arrives in camp with a great school career behind him, a mountain of press clippings, an avalanche of PR, a huge bonus, and a ton of pressure on his back. Fortunately, The Phenom is either too immature to take the pressure seriously or possesses the inordinate cockiness of youth. This means he either fizzles because he doesn't work hard enough or he succeeds after the cockiness ages into confidence and raw ability is rounded by accomplishment.

The Phenom also brings pressure on the team that signs him. The team must quickly bring the kid along to justify the investment and the hype. In the rush to do so, the rising star often burns himself out. Instead of exploding out to radiate greatness throughout the baseball universe, the star implodes. Perhaps the classic case was David Clyde of the Texas Rangers.

Enter Roger Clemens. It's hard to think of Clemens in this light. We think of the pitcher who won an unprecedented seven Cy Young awards and a host of other pitching honors too numerous to mention. We think of the surefire Hall of Famer. Once upon a time, however, Clemens was indeed The Phenom. Boston signed him with fanfare and although great things were predicted, no one knew how it would turn out, especially after arm problems slowed down his first two years in the majors. These many years later, we know how it turned out. The numbers were so good they look liked typos.

I talked with Clemens in March 1984 during his first big league camp. It came after his second Grapefruit League appearance, making it one of the first interviews Roger Clemens did as a major leaguer.

VALENTI: Do you feel pressure coming into camp so highly touted and with so much hype?

CLEMENS: No. The way I look at it, I'm putting more pressure on some of the veterans in camp, just being here and letting them know I'm knocking on the door. That's helping me out by relaxing me, and maybe it's helping them out to get in better shape quicker. So if that's the case, I'm happy. And if that's not the case, then I'm happy too because I'm going to let them know I'm here and ain't nothing can be done to take that away from me, because it's all going to be decided out there on that mound. That's where I want the main stage to be if you're going to judge me. I want it out on the hill. As long as I'm here with the parent club showing what I can do, I'm putting pressure on some other guys and also on the people who have to make the decisions on where I play this year. That's all it's going to take for me to make this club. I just signed and I'm happy to get such a chance so early in my career. I'm not going to waste it.

VALENTI: Did you expect to progress so fast through the Boston system? You shot up in a year.

CLEMENS: I had it in my mind that if I pitched well with [the University of] Texas, I would do well in professional ball. Most baseball people consider pitching for Texas about the same as pitching on a Double A level. And it's about the same, I'd say, judging from my time at New Britain last year. One big difference in professional ball, though, is that they use wooden bats, where in college they used aluminum. That's going to help me, because on a wooden bat, I can come in on hitters and break bats instead of my inside stuff

going for base hits because the aluminum wouldn't break. The biggest change from Double A to the majors is that in the big leagues, I've got to concentrate on all nine hitters. Down in Double A, you really had to bear down on maybe the first six batters and you could ease up a bit on the last three because they were weak hitters. You'd save yourself that way. Up here, every batter can take you out of the park so you gotta concentrate real hard every moment you're out there.

VALENTI: Have you had a chance to see Fenway Park in person?

CLEMENS: Yeah. The Red Sox called me up at the end of last season for 12 games just to give me a look at the park and experience the crowds and everything. I loved the old-timey baseball atmosphere of Fenway. Can't say I'll love that wall in left when I'm out there pitching but seriously, as a fan I loved it. The Sox also brought me up so I could get acquainted with the players and get rid of some of the awe.

VALENTI: After having been there, then, what are your initial thoughts on pitching at Fenway Park?

CLEMENS: Well, people always talk about the short wall in left, but I saw two balls that would have been out of any other park in baseball and only ended up as singles, so I think it keeps as many in as it gives up. I'm sure I'm going to be like anybody else. I've thrown a lot of balls since I've been pitching, and the ones I throw when I miss my location will usually go out of anywhere. That happens with a hard thrower. So I don't think I'll give up a lot of "Fenway homers" and be hurt by the wall. I can't let the wall psyche me out. I just have to pitch like I know I can pitch. If I do that, I'll be OK in Fenway and not waste this opportunity the Red Sox have given me.

VALENTI: How many pitches do you have?

CLEMENS: I have four pitches: a fastball, curve, slider, and change. My changeup is kind of like a split-fingered fastball, but it can work like a forkball too because it will do a little bit of everything. But when I'm throwing hard I like to challenge people, and my fastball's usually my out pitch. I also depend a lot on my curveball. Sometimes in a game it will depend on which pitch is going best for me that day or on the situation and who the batter is. I'm usually a slow starter in the spring, but the last thing to come around usually isn't my fastball but my off-speed stuff. It takes me more time to get it down and I'll need a few more starts. But when I do, it sets off my fastball so that, in most circumstances, my fastball is my out pitch.

VALENTI: How much do you "think" when you're out there on the mound?

CLEMENS: A lot more than most fans realize. You know, pitching is such a thinking game. You gotta keep the batter off his timing and you do that by mixing speeds and doing what he doesn't think you'll do. If you can out-think the batter, he won't out-guess you. But there's only so much thinking you can do. You've got your scouting reports and the different books they keep on batters, and you take all that into account. Then at some point when you're on the mound, you just gotta pitch. I just go to the mound each time confident and sure of myself. I remind myself that all I have to do to win is pitch like I know I can instead of putting pressure on myself and overthrowing or spotting the ball too much. When I try to spot the ball, I usually end up aiming it. When I do that, I lose my velocity. So I just got to make up my mind to go after hitters like I always have.

VALENTI: You are sure to get a lot of media attention this spring. Will that be a distraction? I'm sure you've heard about the Boston press.

CLEMENS: I've heard about the writers up there in Boston, especially if they get on you. But no, y'all in the media won't bother me. At the University of Texas, we got covered big time down there and that's probably the best thing that could have happened to help me adjust to major league writers and the radio and TV people. Plus, I went to two College World Series in my sophomore and junior years. I've pitched in very big games, and that helped me get used to pressure situations and media attention. At Texas there were 30 scouts in the stands each time we played, and that puts a lot of pressure on a young kid. In my sophomore year, I tried to throw the ball through the catcher's mitt just because I knew the scouts were watching. You just try too hard to get attention. The good thing about it is my coach brought me in there and he stayed with me. He just gave me the ball and let me stay in there in pressure games. And I would get stronger as I went along. That happens now. In the sixth or seventh inning, I usually kick in again and pick up a lot of strikeouts. So I think I know how to work out of pressure. Texas, Arizona State, and Miami are the schools they say are on a Double A level. It got me used to things before I got into professional baseball.

VALENTI: [Red Sox manager] Ralph Houk has the reputation of being a pitcher's manager stemming from his days as a catcher. They say he knows how to work a pitching staff. How have you found working for Ralph this spring?

CLEMENS: Ralph's been great. It's very much what you just said about him being a pitcher's manager. You can tell he knows how to talk to us. You can tell he's handled pitchers. He really cares about his staff and he looks out for you. He doesn't overwork you. He looks for anything that might be wrong with what you're doing and anything he can tell you to correct it. He's very observant and doesn't miss anything. Ralph watches us closely and he's told me a couple of things that were helpful to me and that I wanted to know, especially on working certain hitters and also about the need to fully concentrate on the mound each and every pitch. He's talked a lot to me about situations: types of pitches for certain counts, men-on-base situations, who's up and in what spot in the lineup. That's his way of telling me always to concentrate and not let up, especially with the mental aspect of pitching. The main thing for me this spring is that Ralph has expressed confidence in me, saying he's pretty much going to give me the ball. It's up to me to show him what I have.

VALENTI: What kinds of specific things does the coaching staff bring up with you, especially in terms of adjustments?

CLEMENS: The main thing is that they want me to take it easy, that is, not overthrow or think I've got to look great in the Grapefruit League games. I think I had a little tendency to do what I was talking about before, try to throw the ball through the catcher's mitt. The coaches picked up on that and reminded me not to overthrow. It's funny, you think you know that, but when you get all pumped up, this being my first major league spring and all, subconsciously you forget it. There I was, back again in college as a sophomore, trying to impress the scouts. They said I didn't have to do that. Just that alone helped me greatly in calming down. The mechanics and stuff, that's been pretty good.

VALENTI: I've noticed in your sessions on the side that the coaches have seemed pleased with the mechanics, the fluidity of your motion, your release point, and the other technical aspects.

CLEMENS: They've told me that. The key is that I came into camp ready to pitch, because I got into shape early this year to pitch in an alumni game they had in Austin. Then I worked extra hard before I got to Winter Haven, though I think I might have overdone it and started a mite too early. The coaches and Ralph told me not to push too hard. They don't want me hurting my arm or tiring myself out by working too hard, which I have a tendency to do. But it was a big moment for me when Boston invited me to train with the 40-man roster. I realized this was my chance and probably got myself too ready too early. But the coaches have been telling me to relax. They've also been working on me to develop a good, hard slider and to throw at different speeds. They want me to get the exact speed of my changeup where it's supposed to be. They're helping me a lot. I'm a good listener, and I'm going to absorb everything I can.

VALENTI: Do you feel nervous before you start a game?

CLEMENS: Yes. Definitely yes. If I'm not nervous each time I go out there, something's wrong. It's a fine line. I want to feel the nerves but I don't want to feel them too much. I was extremely nervous in my first outing in camp against the Tigers [March 8, 1984]. I was squeezing the ball too hard, my heart was pounding, and that was just natural I guess. That's when Ralph and the coaches talked to me a little about relaxing. They felt they had to step in to calm me down. This time out [after his second start] it wasn't that bad. But I've got to be a little nervous to be at my best, anyway.

VALENTI: You put up great numbers in A ball and Double A last year at Winter Haven and New Britain, respectively. You had ERAs of 1.24 and 1.38. You can't expect the same kind of numbers in Boston, but do you expect an equivalent type of success?

CLEMENS: That's an interesting question. I like the way you put it—"an equivalent type of success." It's something I think a lot about, to be honest. Just how will I do when I get to Boston? I hope I have that type of success. I hope once I get into the swing of things and start to bear down and my off-speed stuff comes around, I would think that I'll have great success in the major leagues. But again to be honest, you never know. I'm just a little bit rusty now with my off-speed stuff, and that usually happens this time of year. The fastball is no problem. That's just rearing back and throwing hard. The off-speed is trickier. My off-speed stuff complements my fastball, making it that much better. If the off-speed stuff comes around and I get my timing right, it'll be that much easier to get my fastball by hitters, and I think I can consistently get my fastball by major league hitters. This year, I'm going to try a new thing. Each day I pitch, I'm going to write down what happens. I'll keep a day-to-day record of what I do against teams and specific hitters. I'll also try to log game situations. I'll see if it helps me learn faster. I think it should. I know I probably won't strike out as many hitters up here on this level because they've seen heat. I mean, they've seen 92-miles-an-hour fastballs in about as many places as you can put it. Plus, major league hitters are more selective. They wait on one pitch they want to see and when they get it they'll hit it. So no doubt. It's going to be a challenge for me to pitch in Boston, but that's the way I like it.

VALENTI: One of the undercurrents of your success and the attention focused on you has been the Red Sox tendency in the past to bring promising young pitchers along too fast or mishandle them in some way. Has this been a concern to you?

CLEMENS: No, it's not a concern. You know, I get compared all the time to what the Rangers did to David Clyde back home in Texas. I've heard that story many times about how they rushed him into the big leagues and how they hurt him. I don't think that can happen to me. I think I'm ready, if they want to rush me they can do it. I'll be ready. If I can prove to the Red Sox that I can handle this challenge, then I want to do it as early as possible. That's not rushing me. That's giving me an opportunity. Remember that David Clyde came into the majors out of high school. I've pitched at the University of Texas, at the A-ball level, and at Double A. Our situations are completely different. I'm not David Clyde. He wasn't Roger Clemens. So I'm not concerned at all about being rushed. I'm ready or at least I think I am. I'm going to give this my best shot, and even if they send me down to Triple A, I'm not going to go down there and pout. I'm going to show them I can pitch up here and that I'm ready. See, if I'm ready they can't rush me. I'm going to work that much harder to get to Boston.

Chapter XI
Images of Spring Past

Carl Yastrzemski poses for the camera on a humid afternoon in the Florida sunshine.
This was taken in 1983, Captain Carl's last year as an active player.

Top, Carney Lansford, American League batting champion in 1981, shares hitting tips with Joe Rudi, left, and Jim Rice that spring. Lower right, Jerry Remy gives it a go in the cage.

Sox second baseman Jerry Remy stretches a point prior to a workout in Winter Haven in 1980, well prior to his reincarnation as Rem Dawg, superb baseball analyst for the Red Sox TV network.

Freeze that ball in mid air, why don't you? Fred Lynn loosens up prior to a Grapefruit game in 1980. Right, Mike Smithson throws and Bruce Hurst watches.

What do you get when you put a football mentality into the body of a baseball player? You get Butch Hobson, who won respect for full-throttle play. Winter Haven, 1981.

Ted Williams takes a hands-on approach with Joe Rudi in the batting cage at the minor league complex, Chain O'Lakes Park, 1981. When it came to hitting, the world stood still when Ted spoke. See Chapter VIII for the full details of this epic hitting lesson.

Dennis Eckersley gets ready to throw from the practice mound under the gaze of Sox pitching coach Johnny Podres. Jim Rice is "at bat."

Eck cuts loose. Note the background. Fans loved hanging out along the diagonal fence, watching the hurlers warm up. Regulars called that area of Chain O'Lakes Park "The Slope." Winter Haven, 1982.

Bruce Hurst, top, and Bob Stanley work on their form in 1984.

Don Zimmer, baseball Buddha, in the dugout at Winter Haven in 1980, his last year as Red Sox manager. Look at this picture, and you'll never wonder why they called him Popeye. Zim was class all the way. No gerbil did I detect.

Dennis Eckersley peers in for the sign, 1982. No, wait, he's peering in at me.

Sox lefty Frank Tanana uncorks, 1981.

Two Legends and long-time friends, intersecting once again.
The Cowboy at the Mike, Curt Gowdy, and Ted Williams,
chat in the visitors' dugout prior to filming a commercial,
Winter Haven, 1982. Hi, neighbor! Have a 'Gansett.

Top left. Wunderkind he wasn't, but for a couple of springs in the early 1980s, shortstop Julio Valdez intrigued observers with his potential. Oh, the curse of potential. Lower right, Skip Lockwood, another bust, points the way to Baseball Beach, 1980.

Jim Rice awaits, stick in hand, Winter Haven, 1980. No one could turn on a ball faster than Rice.

Young Roger Clemens, phenom, gives one of the first TV interviews in his wet-green career, Winter Haven, 1984.

Manager Ralph Houk talks hitting with slugger Jim Rice, 1981.

The Iron Major watches from behind the batting cage. I spent many enjoyable afternoons talking baseball with the Ralph Houk. He could give scribes the "what for," but he never failed a request from this writer.

Bob Stanley, left, gets in some light tossing. Mike Easler, right, calls out infield instructions.

Ralph Houk, man with a bat, on cigarette patrol.
Lower right, Jerry Remy sneaks a smoke in the
dugout during an exhibition game, 1981.

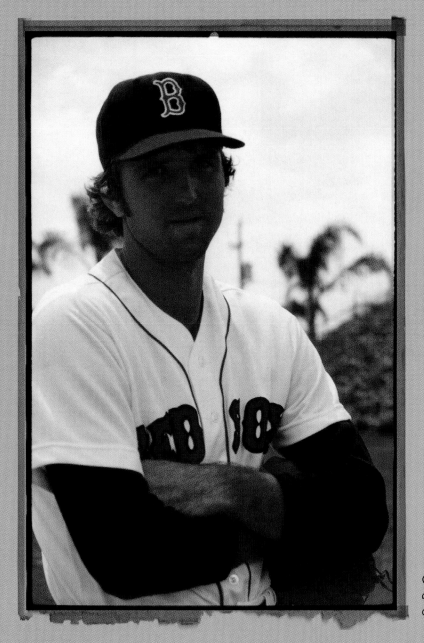

Glenn Hoffman took over shortstopping duty after Rick Burleson bolted in a contract dispute.

Jack Brohamer, 1980. Ever-gracious Jack went out of his way to make this rookie baseball writer feel at home in camp that year.

I love this shot for the way it captures Carl Yastrzemski's love for the game. Yaz tilts his head back in relief and joy. This was taken in the spring of his final year, 1983.

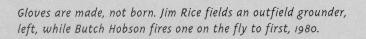

Gloves are made, not born. Jim Rice fields an outfield grounder, left, while Butch Hobson fires one on the fly to first, 1980.

Dave Stapleton, 1981.

The Splendid Splinter poses for the umpteenth time. Ted was at his most
relaxed when making the rounds as an instructor in spring training.

Action around the batting cage,
Winter Haven, 1981. Wade Boggs is
at bat. Frank Malzone leans on a
bat. Glenn Hoffman waits his turn.
Bottom, pitching adviser/coach
Charlie Wagner supervises a
farmhand's throwing session
on the lower fields.

Left, top to bottom. Reid Nichols leads from third, Rick Burleson works on agility drills, and Glenn Hoffman turns a DP, 1981. Right, Jerry Remy proves he's a Jack of all Trades as he throws BP. Is there anything he can't do?

77

Big shoes to fill, 1980, as the Red Sox found out the following year when Carlton Fisk left the team on a technicality after the front office goofed on his contract. Today, Pudge is back in the fold. He went into Cooperstown wearing a Sox cap.

Pudge Fisk looks on, 1980.

Glenn Hoffman takes a grounder during infield drills, 1982. Bottom left, the chap in the green hat was a fixture every St. Patrick's Day at Chain O'Lakes.

Top, Jerry Remy and Jim Rice
get warm. Bottom, Yaz and
Evans get in some long toss.
Winter Haven, 1981.

The smile of a champ. Perennial batting champion Wade Boggs grins behind the cage, 1984.

Carney Lansford guards the hot corner while Tony Perez lunges for a hot smash past first, 1981.

Wade Boggs, Mike Easler, and Dwight Evans put on a pre-game show, Chain O'Lakes Park, Winter Haven, 1982.

Yaz launches an opposite-field hit. Dave Stapleton shags a pop-up in Grapefruit League action, 1983.

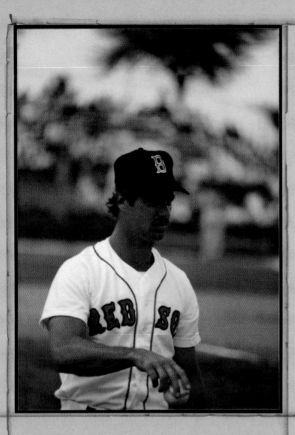

Left, Rick Burleson loads up. Right, the view
from behind the batting cage, 1980.

Top, Rick Burleson and Fred Lynn, deep in thought, 1980. Bottom left, Yaz works out the kinks, 1982. Right, Mike Torrez, Mark Clear, and Man's Best Friend get in their running. The orange groves in the background are long gone, replaced by condos, sad to say.

Manager Ralph Houk readies his lineup.

BOSTON RED SOX
LINEUP CARD

DATE 3-14-81

	BOSTON RED SOX			OPPONENTS
1	Remy	4	**1**	
2	Stapleton	5	**2**	
3	Evans	9	**3**	
4	Rice	7	**4**	
5	Perez	3	**5**	
6	Lansford	@	**6**	
7	Hoffman	6	**7**	
8	Allenson	2	**8**	
9	Nichols	8	**9**	

	LH	EXTRA	RH	LH	EXTRA	RH
	Hancock	Liebert				
	Yaz	Schmidt				
	Miller					
	Gedman					
	LaMacaw	Valdez				
	Aponte	Walter				

No pepper, but there was always plenty of spice and zest when Ted Williams was on the scene. The Kid is seen here with his cue cards during the filming of a TV spot, 1982.

Running, running, and more running.
Bottom, Dwight Evans goes heels over head, 1984.

90

Top, Dennis Eckersley probably drew combat pay for filming this TV commercial in the swamps on the edge of Lake Lulu...where 'gators lurked! Bottom, Dan Valenti grills Yaz on the finer points as John Lickert looks on (photo by Bruce Weber). Right, Yaz recovers from the interrogation, 1983.

Shortstops: one that was, one that never was to be...Julio Valdez, left, and Rick Burleson.

Left, Frank Malzone, Red Sox third base great.
Right, Mark "The Bird" Fydrich flexes his muscles, 1981.

All dressed up and going to the game. Walt Hriniak, Luis Aponte, Glenn Hoffman, Tom Poquette, and manager Ralph Houk, 1981. Bottom, Dwight Evans gives a glove to Fred Lynn, 1980.

Jerry Remy fraternizes with the Twins enemy, 1981.
End of the inning, as Jim Rice has made the last out
in a Grapefruit League tilt, 1982.

Joe Rudi takes his hacks, 1981.

Coach Rac Slider delivers to Roger LaFrancois, 1981.

The Kid, toweling down, 1982.
He even did that with class.

Reid Nichols lays downs a bunt, 1980. Bottom, Dwight Evans slides in safely with a double, 1981.

Mike Torrez goes overhand in synch with Mark Clear, behind him. The Citrus Dome,
a Winter Haven landmark, hovers in the distance.

Top, Gary Allenson obliges a young fan with an autograph. Bottom, Rick Miller looks at one wide. 1981.

Jerry Remy makes with his Casey at the Bat. Reid Nichols catches while Fred Lynn looks on, bemusedly, 1980. Bottom, Gary Allenson, reaching for the tools of ignorance, had the near-impossible job of replacing Carlton Fisk in 1981.

Mark Clear throws BP in the lower fields, left, while Carl Yastrzemski conducts a hitting clinic in the batting cage outside the Red Sox clubhouse, 1983.

Frank Tanana spins off a curve, 1981.

Yaz steps in, left, while Glenn Hoffman makes for second, 1982. The first base coach is Tommy Harper, Luis Tiant's favorite stool pigeon.

105

The media does its job. Voice of the Red Sox Ken Coleman tapes a pre-game show with Carl Yastrzemski, 1983. Ken was a dear friend and a great man.

Glenn Hoffman answers the question, 1982.

Mike Easler waits for the return throw, 1981.

*Jim Rice hustles into the dugout. In the
background, Jerry Remy finds a laugh
with Tommy Harper, 1981.*

Left, Ted Williams shows how it's done, March 10, 1981. Look at the intensity on Ted's face as he launches into this phantom swing. Top right, Frank Malzone watches Ted demonstrate his swing for Joe Rudi. Bottom, The Splinter gives Sox rookie Roger LaFrancois a look-see. See Chapter VIII for the story of this great hitting lesson on the lower fields, Winter Haven, 1981.

"Let me see your swing," Ted tells this lucky youngster. Sam Mele and Eddie Popowski
are in the background, 1981.

Ralph Houk at a press conference, his ever-present bowl of peanuts and soda at the ready, 1981.

Jim Rice shows his classic form, Winter Haven, 1980. He had juice in that bat.

Carl Yastrzemski, The Man they call Yaz, 1983.

Yaz picks out his lumber, 1983.
It was his last spring as a player.

The Dragon, Dick Drago, 1981.

Philosopher Carlton Fisk plays "self-pepper," left,
and salutes the flag during the National Anthem, 1980.

*Jim Rice, 1982. Hall of Famer?
No question. He belongs in
Cooperstown.*

The mercurial Dennis "Oil Can" Boyd enjoys some down time against the fence, 1985.

Johnny Pesky, Mr. Red Sox, leads a work out, 1981.
Bottom, Dwight Evans pulls into third. Eddie Yost
signals, "Hold it right there, Dewey," 1982.

Top, Ned Martin and Bob Montgomery broadcasting back to the fans up north, 1981. Bottom, Ned with hat in hand. Ned brought a rare combination of grace, intelligence, and wit to his "pictures, descriptions, and accounts" of the game. He was the best. Mercy!

.344 lifetime, .406 in 1941, War Hero, the real life John Wayne, and the Greatest Hitter of All Time. What more do you want? He called me "old man." Winter Haven, 1982.

Tom Poquette, looking back, 1983.

Jim Rice, 1982.

Enjoying a light moment, 1983. From left, Yaz, Tony Perez, Dwight Evans (kneeling), Tommy Harper, and Jim Rice.

There's a lot of baseball wisdom being exchanged here. Tommy Lasorda and Don Zimmer, 1980.

Bob Stanley makes the play during one of spring training's endless fielding drills, 1984.

The Iron Major, ready to talk baseball, left, and actually doing it, bottom right, 1983.

Carl Yastrzemski with his lumber, 1983.

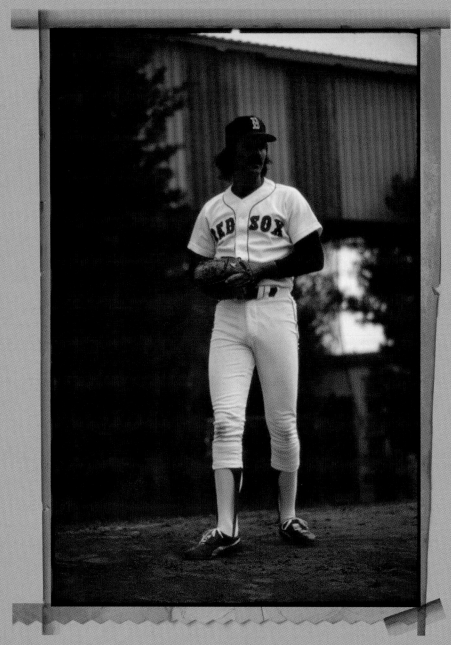

Dennis Eckersley winds up, 1982.

The Eck with Bob Montgomery, 1980.

Ted Williams and Joe Rudi peer in
from behind the batting cage; bottom,
The Kid with Julio Valdez, 1981.

"Joe, make sure you get a good pitch to hit," Ted Williams tells Joe Rudi, March 10, 1981.

Skip Lockwood, 1980, free-agent bust.

Carl Yastrzemski awaits his turn in batting practice, 1983. Every ounce a Hall of Famer, no one outworked Yaz or made more of their God-given abilities.

The pitchers get in their drills, 1980.

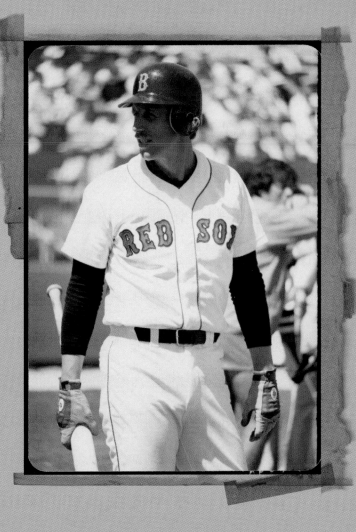

"Broadway" Charlie Wagner conducts class with a Double A prospect on the lower fields at Chain O'Lakes, Winter Haven, 1981. Right, Joe Rudi ready to step up to the plate, 1981.

Tony Perez eases into a throw. Bottom right, hitching a ride, 1981.

He rocks, he throws...Frank Tanana rears back, 1981.

A classic with a classic. Sox legend Johnny Pesky
reads my first book, Red Sox: A Reckoning, 1980.
The book made its way through camp that
year and became my calling card with the
Red Sox organization. Right, Don Zimmer finds
that last question a head scratcher.

Ah, the tough life of a baseball writer.
This is the author, poolside, at the
Landmark Motor Lodge in 1981 (photo
by Bruce Weber). Bottom right, my
long-time friend and business partner,
Ken Coleman, with his new sidekick,
Joe Castiglione.

Red Sox great Frank Malzone, 1980. Bottom, the gear piles up, left, while Ralph Houk confers with Haywood Sullivan, 1981. They were discussing the loss of Carlton Fisk to a contractual boo-boo by the front office. Neither Sully nor Houk were too happy that day.

pete runnels

BOSTON RED SOX
SECOND BASE

Heads Up: Pete Runnels, shown fielding an imaginary grounder on his 1959 Topps baseball card, a combination of lowbrow baseball and high commercial art. Dig the pink background. What has this to do with us? See Chapter VI, "The Pink of Pistol Pete," page 21.

Carl Yastrzemski reflects back on his long career during an interview in 1983.